TO KNOW SWEET YOU MUST TASTE SOUR

A Cancer Survivors Self-Help Guide

By

DIANE FINNEY

Reflections from a Breast Cancer Survivor on how to Enjoy Life!

Copyright © 2014 by Diane Finney

ISBN: 069223747X
ISBN-13: 978-0692237472

Published by MacGuffin Press
www.dianefinney.com
Printed in the United States of America

ALL RIGHTS RESERVED

No part of this publication may be reproduced, stored in a retrieval system or transmitted in any form or by any means without the prior written permission of the publisher.

MacGuffin Press and associated logos are trademarks and/or registered trademarks of MacGuffin Press.

Photography and Image Credits: Diane Finney, Chris Finney

Cataloging-in-Publication Data is on file with the Library of Congress.

At the time of this book's publication, all facts and figures are current. Some names and identifying details have been changed to protect the privacy of individuals. The author, Diane Finney and MacGuffin Press make no warranty or guarantee concerning information or materials given out by organizations thru websites mentioned in this book and are not responsible for any changes that occur on their websites after publication of this book. The purpose of this book is to enlighten and educate the reader. This book is not intended as a substitute for the medical advice of physicians. The reader should regularly consult a physician in matters relating to his/her health and particularly with respect to any symptoms that may require diagnosis or medical attention. The author, editors and publisher shall have neither liability or responsibility to anyone with respect to any loss or damage caused or alleged to be caused, directly or indirectly by the information contained in this book.
Editors: Diane Finney, Chris Finney
Cover design by Robert Finney
Book design and production done with the Epub Template

Dedication

*I would like to dedicate this book in loving memory
to my mother, Lois Wisti Cruikshank
1926 — 2014
Mom, your upbeat spirit and bravery in the face
of adversity will inspire me forever.*

Endorsements

"Anyone who picks up this book will find it truly inspiring & amazing."

– **Lynn Bottger,** USPTA tennis pro

"As a cancer survivor I can appreciate the insider information that Diane shares in her book. I found for myself and others that I help, that the scariest time after being told you have the "Big C" is between diagnosis and the start of treatment. Confusion and fear over whelm you and you do not know what to ask and who to ask it of. Diane's book shares her same journey, answering questions and concerns as she travels back to recovery."

– **KT Budde-Jones,** cancer survivor.

"It is with tremendous admiration for Diane's strength, courage and generosity of spirit in sharing her experiences with cancer that I recommend "To Know Sweet You Must Taste Sour". There is an overwhelming amount of available technical information on dealing with the illness, but a huge need for this type of personal testimonial that will help any patient know that it is possible to cope with cancer with grace, style and humor. Research confirms that a positive approach and strong ties to family and friends are of enormous value to recovery. Diane offers a blueprint for positivity culled from her hard won experience."

> **– Kimberly Kirschner,** Certified Food for Life Instructor for The Cancer Project & PCRM.org, A4M Fellow, Integrative Oncology

"I am an oncologist - a cancer specialist. I see cancer patients every day, in fact, Diane is one of my patients. Although each patient is surrounded by doctors, nurses, family, each must ultimately face their cancer alone. This book is Diane's version of how she dealt with her cancer. It is not a recipe, but rather, her approach to the many problems she faced and how she overcame them. Read it, copy those ideas that may work for you, discuss it with your family. Just as there are many kinds of cancer, there are many ways to get through having cancer. Good Luck!!"

> **– Lee M. Zehngebot,** M.D

"In a matter of only a few days after having a double mastectomy, Diane Finney traveled with hometown friends for a 3-day women's only excursion to NYC. The short venture included attendance at multiple Broadway shows, sight-seeing expeditions, the official Christmas tree lighting ceremony, fine dining and teas. Throughout the extremely active days, we were in awe of Diane's high level of energy, her adventurous excitement and chronic state of happiness. I wondered what could be the 'secret' for such an upbeat spirit; I wondered, that is, until I read Diane's book "To Know Sweet You Must Taste Sour". The book is a delightful read, laced with Diane's unique humor and complete with a host of suggestions helpful in maintaining an optimistic, upbeat attitude throughout and beyond the cancer ordeal. As a survivor of breast cancer, the book had a significant impact upon my own perspective of the disease, changing my attitude from one of repressed fear to that of sincere gratitude for the opportunity to touch, feel and appreciate life as never before. The book is a must read for cancer survivors and caregivers, as well." **– Cynthia Buffington,** PhD

Dear Reader,

Friends of mine, who watched me deal with Breast Cancer, twice within seven years, were amazed by the positive attitude I projected and the fortitude I displayed. The meaning of fortitude from the Merriam-Webster dictionary is **Fortitude:** *Strength of mind that enables a person to encounter danger or bear pain or adversity with courage.* If it is true that dealing with adversity builds character then I think that experiencing cancer makes us much more interesting people.

My friends encouraged me to express my thoughts and share my words of advice with those of you out there who might be facing similar health challenges. So, if you could use a pep talk, I think you will find my little book to be uplifting. I chose the title **To Know Sweet, you must Taste Sour,** because sometimes it takes experiencing something bad to appreciate the good things in life. One thing is for sure; you will never take good health for granted again. You only live life once, so make it the best you can! I wrote this book to help people beat this dreaded disease. It is my fond hope that this small volume proves helpful to you.

Sincerely,

Diane Finney

P.S. A portion of the profits from the sale of this book will be given to the American Cancer Society.

Table of Contents

Copyright ii

Dedication iii

Endorsements v

Forward xv

Prologue 1

My Speech given at Relay For Life 5

My Health Timeline 9

Chapter 1: Sweet to Sour - taste the contrast 13

Chapter 2: The Pity Party 17

Chapter 3: Lemons 19

Chapter 4: Family Relationships 21

Chapter 5: Friends, Diet and Exercise 25

Chapter 6: The Three P's of Work Purpose, Passion and being Positive 33

Chapter 7: Why me? 37

Chapter 8: Plan of Action 41

Chapter 9: Tips, Nuts and Bolts of Cancer 43

Chapter 10: Pain 51

Chapter 11: Tennis and Golf 55

Chapter 12: The Power of Belief that you
 will get Well 61

Chapter 13: The Bucket List 65

Chapter 14: Depression 69

Chapter 15: Nature Walk 73

Chapter 16: Loss of a Loved One 75

Chapter 17: Strength and Humor 83

Chapter 18: How Cancer made me a
 better Poker Player 87

Chapter 19: Tempting Fate 91

Chapter 20: Seven Stages of Grief as it
 relates to Cancer 95

Chapter 21: Losing Weight 99

Chapter 22: Healthy Choices 101

Chapter 23: Journaling 105

Chapter 24: The Power of Faith 109

Chapter 25: Putting your Affairs in Order 111

Chapter 26: Cancer Events 115

Chapter 27: My Favorite Books 119

Chapter 28: My Favorite Movies 121

Chapter 29: Bottle of Optimism Email 123

Chapter 30: A few words from my Spouse 127

Chapter 31: Marijuana 129

Chapter 32: Summary: Appreciate the
    'Good Things in Life' 133

Acknowledgements 135

About the Author 139

About the Publisher MacGuffin Press 141

Forward

In the autumn of 2004, I attended a party at the home of two people whom I had never met – Chris and Diane Finney. When I saw Diane for the first time, I could not help but notice her short hair and the sporty baseball cap she was wearing. I asked one of her friends if she had had cancer; her friend responded that Diane was fighting breast cancer. As I watched her at this party, I was absolutely amazed at the sincerely positive and exuberant attitude which she radiated in the face of such hardship.

Over the nearly ten years during which I have known Diane, our relationship has always been friendly. For many years, Diane and I worked every month on a newspaper article about an organization in which we were both deeply involved and during that time we were very close. Only once did Diane and I ever discuss her cancer. One evening, over a glass of wine, I asked her about her experiences with cancer. At the time, I thought that her response was odd. It wasn't an answer of avoidance about the past; rather it was an answer of optimism about the future. She was clearly not like others with whom I had spoken who were stuck dwelling on their medical woes. Now, years later, I understand her answer through the pages of *To Know Sweet You Must Taste Sour*.

It is true that I have learned much about Diane from reading her book. I also have learned that what I already knew about her was correct. In this book, a real Renaissance woman (with a "bucket list" that matches) who squeezes the best from every moment which manifests in life is revealed – an emotionally and physically courageous woman who demonstrates the importance of relying on listening, intuition, intellect, faith, and medicine to overcome the fear that anyone who has been diagnosed with a life-threatening illness must feel. We are fortunate that she has decided to share this guidance with us.

What Diane has given us on these pages is a manual for life for anyone who has cancer, anyone who has survived cancer, and all those who seek to help someone who is or has experienced cancer. Diane's good humor, practical approach, positive attitude, and focus on what is important are all here in *To Know Sweet You Must Taste Sour*. The reader leaves inspired to emphasize the positive and reject the negative.

Be warned that this book is so intensely and honestly written that you will invest yourself in Diane's life and, through that experience, find more growth within yourself. I cried about Yoda the cat and Matilda the dog and I laughed out loud about Diane's newfound marijuana hobby. You will be inspired, helped, and changed for the better because you have read Diane's words.

In Chapter 15, Diane has written that she hopes "that my existence had an enriching impact on those around me." Be assured, Diane, that it has for all those who know you and that it will for the many who will now get to know you through this wonderful book.

Diane's friend,
Valleri Crabtree

Prologue

I consider myself to be a fairly typical American woman who grew up in a suburb of Minneapolis, Minnesota. I had never lived anywhere else and so I had a yearning to be adventurous, explore the world and hence; I majored in Anthropology at the University of Minnesota. I met my husband during my senior year of college; we married and had three sons. Didn't you hear that breast feeding your babies was supposed to help prevent breast cancer? Ha, ha, ha! Well, years later I found out that breast feeding didn't work for me!

I enjoyed ten years of being a stay at home Mom and then returned to work part-time at a variety of occupations. During those wonderful years of raising our sons, we moved to Massachusetts and then returned to Minnesota and finally job opportunities led us to Florida. I was active with volunteering in the boy's schools and in our community – middle class, clean living at its best. Growing up I was considered an athletic tom boy and I remained physically active in sports. I was healthy as a horse and had no reason or family history to give me a premonition of what was to come.

At age forty-six I recall getting stung by an insect and then coming down with a sore throat while we were on a cruise chaperoning my son's high school tennis team. I felt so lousy that I actually bought some antibiotics in Belize to try and kill the infection. A week after returning from the cruise, I found an egg sized lump under my right arm pit. We hoped that it was just a swollen lymph node from the cold I had been fighting.

It turned out to be a cancer in my right breast that had aggressively spread to my lymph nodes. As you will see in the following chapters, this was just the beginning of my battle with cancer. Friends have been amazed at how I managed to be upbeat and not lose my cool.

One of the positive things that has come out of my having cancer is learning more about the American Cancer Society and getting to know the organizers of events that help to raise money to find a cure for cancer. One of the great activities that the American Cancer Society promotes as a fundraiser is Relay For Life. This 12 plus hour event celebrates cancer survivors and honors those who have won or lost their battle with cancer. It is a moving experience to be cheered during the Survivors walk and then to watch the luminaries be lit in remembrance of loved ones who are no longer with us. Teams compete in a friendly manner to see who can raise the most funds as they take turns walking the Relay course throughout the night.

My attitude and cancer surviving experience impressed the organizers of Relay For Life and they asked me to give the opening speech for our community event. The following is the speech I gave.

My Speech given at Relay For Life

Hello, I'm Diane Finney and I'm a Cancer Survivor times two. Eight years ago I discovered an Easter egg sized lump under my right armpit. It literally appeared overnight. Up to then, I thought I was healthy but imagine my surprise when doctors told me I had an aggressive form of Breast Cancer. Why me? I couldn't believe it! Was this a cruel joke being played on me? There wasn't any history of cancer in my family; I was clueless about Cancer. But, I followed doctors' orders and I was a poster child for the Lumpectomy, Chemotherapy and Radiation treatment on my right breast. All told, it was pretty easy for me, I never felt sick but I did lose my hair. Hoping to be done with Cancer forever, I asked the Doctors to "Bring it on," for the last chemo cocktail, which I handled just fine.

After 7 Cancer free years, many of my friends thought I was 'out of the woods' that I had nothing to worry about.

Not. Unknown to me, Cancer had come back. A friend said that Cancer hides in fat so a year ago I decided to become more fit and lose some weight. I should have done this years ago but better late than never! I want you to know that my decision to get healthy may have saved my life. Because I had become thinner, the good doctors at Celebration Hospital spotted some cancer cells in my left breast during my mammogram exam. It was a different form of cancer that left undiscovered is the type that spreads all over. So I underwent a double Mastectomy with Reconstruction. Some people handle their Cancer with learning all they can about it. I will admit, I'm not one of those people. It's not that I put my head in the ground but I just feel that Cancer has dominated enough of my life and so I choose not to study it. I'm happy to say that 6 weeks after surgery I was back to playing tennis and golf. Ah, the choices we make.

So you know how Cancer changes your life? You appreciate each day like never before. You might play a lousy round of Golf or Bridge but it is still a beautiful day. Cancer makes you prioritize and take charge of your life. Live in the Now! You move things you wish to do from the back burner to the front and create a Bucket List of goals. Even though I'm an optimist, Cancer has heightened my appreciation for life. Try to think of the Ups and Downs of your Cancer experience as being introduced to a new food. Without taste buds, life would have fewer flavors. You would not fully appreciate joy without experiencing the contrast of sadness. Friends have been amazed at my positive attitude and have urged me to write a book about how I have dealt with Cancer. This self-help guide I'm working on is entitled "To Know Sweet, you must Taste Sour." So on my Bucket List is getting my various novels published, creating more Art, traveling to exotic places and I also want to win a World Series of Poker bracelet. Just a modest **Wish** list, I know.

I'd like to say word or two about Caregivers: I have been lucky to have family and friends who have offered their help or expressed their sincere wishes for a speedy recovery and a successful victory in my battle against cancer. The fact is that I couldn't fight the good fight without these wonderful people cheering me on. I'd like to give a **Big Thank You** to my husband Chris and my sons Robert, Nick and Jack for their loving support during both bouts of Breast Cancer. I'd like to thank my long distance friends and family members who cheered me up with their Get Well cards and flowers. And I would like to thank all my friends in Celebration for their kind words and assistance, you know who you are! As we walk through life, it is the helping hand of a friend that enhances our journey and there is no better place to walk than Celebration. I'd like to say that the entire community of Celebration has been very supportive of me – I can't say **Thank You** enough!

And so I stand here before you with a new appreciation of being alive! Besides raising money to fight cancer and find a cure, I know why we are here at Relay For Life: it is to honor the courage of those dealing with cancer and to acknowledge the role of the caregivers in our lives and express our appreciation and love to them.

Tennis player Maria Bartoli recently said, "Quitters never Win, Winners never quit." I think that is a good thought to keep in mind as we participate in Relay For Life.

There is a Scandinavian word "Skol" which means "cheers," or "good health," and it is said as a salute to an admired person or group. And so I would like to end our time together with a sincere toast to every Cancer Survivor and Caregiver, with us here today or in our memory – **"Skol!"**

My Health Timeline

2004 – April

I discovered the egg sized lump under my right armpit. Doctors find another tumor in my right breast, close to my chest wall. It turns out to be a Stage 2 Triple Negative Breast Cancer. I agree to lumpectomy surgery, commence chemotherapy and finish up with radiation of my right breast area by mid - November.

2011 – March

I saw some unflattering photos taken of me – it was shocking how I had let myself go! Knowing that cancer hides in fat, I start to seriously diet and lose weight.

September

During my annual mammogram, a doctor discovers what looks like a tiny broken string of seed pearls in my left breast. A biopsy reveals it is estrogen positive Stage 0 Breast Cancer. Because I have now had two different forms of breast cancer, it is recommended that I have a double mastectomy. In my case, nipple saving surgery is not a good idea. It's suggested that I consider having my ovaries removed.

November

I have the double mastectomy surgery with skin saving for breast reconstruction implants. During surgery to remove both breasts, tumors on the outer fringe of my left breast are discovered making me Stage 1. If I had not had the double mastectomy… those estrogen positive tumors contain the cancer cells that can spread throughout the body. For the next 5 years I will be taking a pill (Femara) that is an aromatase inhibitor. I will also be taking a calcium and fish oil pills to counteract the calcium depleting side effects of Femara.

2012 – January to April

Every other week or so I would go to the plastic surgeon's office for implant expansion. Hope to become a full C cup.

May

Semi-permanent implant plastic surgery. Rather than just having my ovaries removed, it is recommended that I consider a complete hysterectomy. I meet with several doctors to get various opinions.

September

Not pleased with the way things are progressing with the plastic surgery, I replaced that doctor and meet with a new plastic surgeon recommended by my oncologist. I also consult with a genetic counselor and finally get my insurance company to cover the costs of doing the BRAC 1 and 2 tests. It turns out to be negative. Still trying to decide about doing the hysterectomy, I have a pelvic ultrasound done and a mass is discovered in my cervix. In a heartbeat I schedule the complete hysterectomy to be done with the da Vinci robotics method.

November

Complete hysterectomy surgery.

2013 - January

Plastic surgery for breast reconstruction and fat graft. In the spirit of turning a negative into a positive I also have a tummy tuck done.

May

Consultation with the plastic surgeon for additional breast reconstruction later in the year. Nipple reconstruction remains a possibility. At the very least, I can get a three dimensional tattoo to mimic nipples.

October

I meet with the plastic surgeon. We had hoped that given more time the tight skin covering my breasts might give a little more. As I understood it; if my breast skin was stretched too taut, there was a risk of implant eruption through the surgical incisions. When my husband heard that I thought he would faint. My dear husband of 32 years of marriage tried to discourage me from considering any further surgery. He was happy with the way I looked and didn't want me to risk what I had already accomplished.

We discussed the options and I asked the plastic surgeon that if he was in my shoes; what would he do? His answer was he'd go for it. His optimism matched mine but I decided to give myself a few days to think it over. A few days later I decided to continue with my breast reconstruction and so I had nipples created out of the skin covering my breast implants.

So far, so good. Three months from the surgery I plan to return for a couple of tattoos! To date; I remain a work in progress.

CHAPTER I

Sweet to Sour – taste the contrast

I'm going to share with you my experience in dealing with breast cancer and maintaining a positive attitude. You might ask; how is it possible to be at all positive when dealing with adversity? In my self help guide book I will share with you tips and things to do to help you through your health challenge.

First, I'd like to explain the concept behind the title of this book, **To Know Sweet You Must Taste Sour**. I'm going to describe experiencing adversity in terms of the senses because it all comes down to a matter of perception and being able to apply your will power to maintain a positive attitude.

The traditional five senses are: hearing, smell, touch, sight and taste. Recently I attended an alcohol beverage tasting event where the instructor asserted that you taste with all your senses. For example, just hearing a beverage being poured heightens your anticipation of the drink. You might hear the bubbles popping if its champagne you are tasting. Swirl your drink and stick your nose into the glass. Do you smell fruit, wildflowers or exotic spices? Feel the texture of your beverage as you roll it about your tongue. Hold a glass of wine against the light and its color hints at flavors. The deeper the color of the wine, the bolder the flavor. And always be aware of the finish. I believe this perception holds true for your cancer experience too.

Let's concentrate on taste. You are able to taste things such as food through the sensory organs called taste buds on the top surface of your tongue. There are five basic tastes that your taste buds can determine. They are sweet, sour, bitter, salty and umami. You might ask; what is umami? Umami is a pleasant and savory taste in your mouth. Taste buds for sweet, generally thought to be pleasant are to the front. Some researchers would say that humans have been conditioned over time to prefer the pleasurable taste of sweet ripe fruit containing sucrose sugar over the sour flavor of unripe fruit. The sour taste buds which detect acidity are located on the sides of your tongue. If you have ever bitten into a slice of lemon, you might make a prune face (ooooh) that is the acidic tartness you feel in reaction to the sour taste.

Have you ever noticed that when your nose is plugged with a cold, nothing tastes good? Being able to smell combined with taste perception gives you the sense of flavor.

I would argue that if you did not experience the contrast of these taste sensations, sweet opposed to sour; you would not fully appreciate the food in your diet. Taking this a step further as it relates to your life; it is experiencing the worst that can happen that we come to truly appreciate the good things in life. You might have gone on existing with a bland diet, not even aware of how good (sweet) things were without the sharp sour tasting, dark edge of hardship. Having cancer can bring enlightenment to your existence. And so I maintain that it is with experiencing the bad, sour misfortunes in our lives that we gain clarity to recognize and truly appreciate the good, sweetness of life that would not have been possible before.

In the words of former President Richard Nixon, "The greatness comes not when things go always good for you. But the greatness comes when you're really tested, when you take some knocks, some disappointments, when sadness comes. Because only if you've been in the deepest valley can you ever know how magnificent it is to be on the highest mountain."

In the interests of hearing from both political parties, former President Bill Clinton had this reflection to share; "If you live long enough, you'll make mistakes. But if you learn from them, you'll be a better person. It's how you handle adversity, not how it affects you. The main thing is never quit, never quit, never quit."

The contrasting sensations of sweet to sour heighten the flavors of our life experience as individuals. We can now go forward with new knowledge and a positive attitude about the benefits of the cancer experience.

CHAPTER 2

The Pity Party

So you found out that you have Cancer... Foremost of all, the first question that you might ask yourself is: why did I get cancer? Your Oncologist may have some explanation. I don't have an answer for you. Of all the people in the world, you wonder why you had to get Cancer. Could it be poor choices in your diet or bad genes or less than smart health decisions? Who knows?

There are Cancer Support groups you can connect with through your hospital. The old saying is that misery loves company; you are not alone and there are other people out there dealing with cancer that would love to chat. It's understandable to feel sorry for yourself and to seek comfort with others who understand what you are feeling.

These support groups can be helpful for people who want to talk about their situation and sort out their emotions. Check with your local hospital and the American Cancer Society for assistance in finding support groups in your area.

For some people, dwelling on their cancer prognosis becomes a focus of their life. I attended a couple of meetings but for me, it wasn't the way I wanted to spend my time. Time is something I have always scoffed at and never let control me. Now after dealing with Cancer once again, I find time to be a very valuable commodity and I refuse to squander it.

Maybe you can allow yourself a few seconds of self-pity and/or anger at fate. Your sadness may turn into a rage at the injustice of the world. Go ahead and vent if it makes you feel better. But honestly don't waste any more time than that! It is my opinion that life is too short. From this point on make every second count!

CHAPTER 3

Lemons

When life serves you lemons... make lemonade. This is not only a helpful saying but also it expresses a positive attitude to adopt. Being positive will get you through many difficulties that you will face in life.

How often have we heard that expression? Think about it and you realize there is a kernel of truth that everyone should take to heart. Terrible things happen: tragic accidents, meaningless violence, unkind acts done without reason and of course cancer. You may have gone through life forgetting to appreciate the little everyday things such as; the sweet smell of flowers on a wafting breeze, the feel of warm sunshine on your face, birdsong waking you up in the morning, the laughter of children playing nearby, a joke shared amongst friends, a cup of fragrant tea enjoyed as the late afternoon sun slants through the woods. Our own taste buds are ready to interpret the flavors of the food we eat. Sometimes it happens that to recognize the **Sweet** in life, you must experience the **Sour.**

When life gets you down; it is how you meet the challenge that defines your character. In the words of Eleanor Roosevelt, "You gain strength, courage, and confidence by every experience in which you really stop to look fear in the face... do the thing you think you cannot do." I have found that dealing with cancer helps me to prioritize what is important in life to me. Goals I wish to pursue, projects I want to complete are moved from the back burner to the front.

If you are feeling bad, smile. Researchers say that the physical act of smiling releases hormones that make you feel happier. This mysterious phenomenon is one that you can use to your advantage.

In my case, when life served me lemons (double mastectomy)... I made grapefruits! (Reconstructive surgery) So when life throws you a curve ball, be brave, meet the challenge; grin and bear it. Tomorrow is another, better day.

CHAPTER 4

Family Relationships

They say you can't choose your family but you can choose your friends. This is so true. However it doesn't mean that you have to submit and simply remain a victim of fate with your family. Take charge of your time and spend it wisely. That means making choices about your companionship. I am lucky to be married to a very supportive husband who showed me his true colors when I was diagnosed with cancer. Our love and appreciation for each other grew and our marriage became even more rock solid. In one sense, having cancer made us focus on our relationship and we both realize we value our partnership. Cancer made us come to terms with the fact that nothing lasts forever so take joy and comfort in each other, every day.

My husband has been a wonderful caregiver to me but not everyone experiences the strengthening effect that cancer had on our marriage. Several people I know had the sad experience of their spouse actually leaving them because of their illness. I like to think there is a special place in Hell for faithless, bad spouses. Take comfort in believing that what comes around, goes around and these bad people will get their just desserts.

Examine what is good about your family and enjoy it. Incorporate the best elements and ignore the bad. I have three sons who have been there for me, not always at the same time and not even in person but a loving phone call can be just as uplifting to your spirit as a warm hug. If someone makes a mistake - you can choose to be your own person and not copy bad behavior. If you experienced bad parenting, you don't have to repeat it – make a conscious decision to be different. The same goes for children who misbehave as adults. The time has come for the little birds to fly away from the nest and give their parents some well-deserved freedom. You can choose to spend your valuable time and holidays with other people; people who exert positive vibes. Or you can use your cancer as an opportunity to mend fences and build bridges to a more positive relationship. Maybe you should bury the hatchet.

TO KNOW SWEET YOU MUST TASTE SOUR

Limit your exposure to negative family members or friends who cause stress and poison your life. If stress causes cancer then some situations and certain people are hazardous to your health! It's your right to avoid stress so focus on being with people that will make you healthier.

Regarding in-laws and family members, relationships can improve. Sometimes the shock that you have cancer can actually cause these in-laws and/or family members to re-evaluate your relationship. There is no time like today to mend fences, extend olive branches and forgive. You can use your cancer as a springboard to build bridges to a more positive relationship. It might well be time to say "let bygones be bygones." Whatever the reality of your experience, remember to look out for yourself, be ever hopeful and trust your instincts. Perhaps the best is yet to be!

CHAPTER 5

Friends, Diet and Exercise

Some good advice I once received from a relative when I had moved to a new part of the country was to cultivate friends. Friends are extremely important as a support group. You should reach out to them and let them know what you are going through. Sometimes a friendship can be sparked with another person dealing with cancer. It's very easy to talk to someone who is in your same boat.

At the same time, you might find that some friends actually take a step back from you. They might have the misconception that cancer is contagious. These things happen and just don't dwell on the loss of a friend if they act aloof. Give them time to adjust to your new health situation and they might come around and your relationship will be better for it. If these so-called friends continue to ignore you, then say good riddance to false friends and hug the people who are supportive. Both new and old friends should be cultivated, handled with care and treasured forever.

Exercise is a great stress reliever. If you are not part of a walking group – form one of your own. A doctor once said that if he could give one piece of advice that would improve your quality of life it would be to go outside, shut your front door and walk for a mile and a half. Then turn around and walk back. Three miles a day would do wonders for your health!

There is nothing like fresh air to clear your head of various issues and help you to concentrate on the important things in life such as walking and talking with friends. It's amazing how talking about what is bothering you can help to lighten your day. Time and the miles you walk pass very quickly when you are engaged in an interesting discussion.

A couple of years ago, I was very fortunate to be asked to join a Tuesday morning Walk & Talk group. Every Tuesday we would meet and walk about our community and discuss various issues or whatever was troubling us. Friendships strengthened and the sense of camaraderie was so positive that we gradually attracted more amazing ladies.

One of the walk group gals was going through chemo treatment for an unusual and aggressive type of breast cancer (triple negative). We bonded immediately when I shared with her my story of having breast cancer about six years previously. The group's consensus was that I was golden; I was out of the woods. My new friend wanted to know what kind of breast cancer I had been treated for, but I had no idea.

You see, people handle these health challenges differently. My friend became an expert on types of breast cancer, various treatment options, new research etc. I preferred to not make cancer a focus of my life, nor study it. I felt that just dealing with cancer had taken up enough of my time and energy. Do you believe in the power of your mind? I do and I believed that thinking about cancer would give it more life, more power and influence. Why give cancer any more attention and thereby extend its importance? I preferred to focus my attention on other areas of interest; art, writing, gardening, playing poker, etc. I trusted my doctors to be trained professionals who would use their medical knowledge to treat and cure me of cancer.

To satisfy my friend's curiosity I promised to find out what kind of breast cancer I had dealt with six years earlier when I saw my oncologist at the next scheduled visit. I asked him and to my amazement, I learned that I had the same triple negative type of breast cancer that my friend had told me was so aggressive and dangerous. Well, there's a saying that ignorance is bliss. I was happy being in the dark but now I was enlightened to the actual deadliness of the breast cancer the doctors had removed and treated with chemo and radiation. At that time I had been six plus year's cancer free and many people thought that I had nothing to worry about.

Don't keep what is bothering you, to yourself. Write it down in a journal or talk it through with someone. I wrote this guide book to help people deal with adversity in a positive way. If you are angry about something, keeping it bottled up can create stress; and stress they (medical authorities) say may cause cancer. So lighten your load and share your fears and hopes with your walking buddies.

During a holiday visit with my sons, they asked to see their old baby pictures. While searching for those, I came across a photo album of our ten year wedding anniversary cruise. I was shocked to see a terrific photo of me looking fit and trim. I took a hard look at myself in the mirror and was dismayed to see how heavy I looked in comparison to the photo taken of me at age 33. I am an avid tennis player but I appeared to have grown larger despite occasional efforts to diet. I knew I had gotten heavier but wouldn't daily exercise have combated getting overweight? Truth be told, over the last couple of years I'd realized my pants size was increasing, my sporadic efforts to lose some weight had failed. The results were disappointing.

How had this weight gain happened? I knew I had enjoyed too many cruises and over eating in the years since my first bout of cancer, seven years before. When friends and loving relatives realized I was going thru cancer treatment, many wanted to show they cared by taking me out for lunch or dinner. I never turned anyone down. I'm afraid my attitude was a bit of 'Eat, Drink and be Merry for tomorrow we Die' and that lifestyle had finally caught up with me. Years of self-indulgence had packed on the weight. I decided to slim down.

I'd also heard from friends and medical authorities the news that cancer hides in fat. Realizing that I once had the aggressive triple negative breast cancer helped me to take losing weight seriously. I consulted with my oncologist and the physician's assistant for dieting guidance and became determined to change my lifestyle and lose some weight.

If you want to lose weight; I'll tell you the secret.... It's simple – eat less and exercise more. While I dieted, I increased my level of exercise by doing more of the activities I already loved. Tennis, golf, gardening and walking are my favorite things to do. My husband and I already played tennis first thing in the morning before work so it was easy to add another set of tennis in the late afternoon or evening. Another tip; drink lots of water. As your body burns up the fat, the water will help to flush it out of your system. I discovered that as I saw improvement, I was encouraged to keep going. Friends began to notice and I got a few compliments which added fuel to my desire to shed pounds and years off my reflection in the mirror. I am convinced that determination to watch what you eat and exercise more strengthens your character. In the words of Oprah Winfrey, "Where there is no struggle, there is no strength." I was successful in losing about 1/5 of my body weight – yahoo!

But the real benefit of losing weight was that it probably saved my life. During my next mammogram appointment, the doctor spotted tiny tumors, like a string of broken pearls in my left breast. A biopsy revealed that the tiny dots were cancer; a different kind than before. This breast cancer was estrogen positive and I am so grateful that it was spotted by the doctor with the great eyesight; because this cancer is the kind that spreads throughout your body. It is my sincere belief that because I had gotten thinner, the cancer was spotted and could not remain hidden inside me to multiply out of control. Thank heavens for the good eyesight and professionalism of the mammogram technicians!

Some things are out of your control but not a change in attitude about adopting a healthy lifestyle. I was recently introduced to the healthful benefits of juicing and blending up fruit and vegetable concoctions. It can't hurt and by eating more natural and organic foods you might help your body to cure itself. Those original juicer advocates seem to live to ripe old ages. Just keep in mind that moderation is the key. That is so true for many things.

At a recent Relay For Life event, a doctor at our local hospital (Florida Hospital, Celebration) spoke about the benefits of exercise and cancer survival. Their research is already showing that exercise can help to prevent cancer and will help you to fight it as part of your treatment.

Recent news reports have brought attention to breast cancer survivors healing through exercise. Some fitness trainers have offered free group classes to cancer survivors. They find a common bond with each other that could help make all the difference in their recovery. As a breast cancer survivor you become a member of a club that you might never have wanted to join. But by becoming physically active with others who share similar health concerns you will have a camaraderie that makes all the difference in your life going forward.

My advice: if you are overweight, consult with your doctor about diets and get serious about shedding some pounds. Losing excess weight and exercising will be beneficial in so many ways and you will be denying cancer a place to hide.

CHAPTER 6

The Three P's of Work Purpose, Passion and being Positive

How do you define work? Or does your work define you? I'm sure you have heard that if you love your job; you will never work a day in your life.

That being said, many of us find ourselves stuck in jobs that are not fulfilling... unless getting a paycheck is all you are asking for in life. I have worked many tedious jobs, one comes to mind where I stamped numbers onto pieces of paper all day and then put them in order and filed them away... Fortunately I didn't stay in that occupation for too long or I might be brain dead today. Sometimes I found myself working at a job just for a vacation... not very satisfying when all is said and done. So examine what you are doing to make a living and assess how close that is to what you really want to do. Then figure out a way to pursue your dream because life is too short.

Personality and Occupation Assessment Tests are available to help you narrow down your options and determine what occupation you should pursue. Myers Briggs is one that comes to mind that might assist you to better understand your personality and to point you in the right vocational direction.

Vocation or avocation? A young lawyer once told me he would rather be painting but his work as an attorney paid for a good lifestyle. It allowed him the money to buy paint supplies to dabble in art when he had time. At that point in his life he seemed to have come to terms with the tradeoff between having a good income versus being artistically creative.

To find a satisfying occupation – to discover your **Purpose**; you must examine what you are **Passionate** about. Give yourself time to do some deep thinking because how you spend your time in life is important. Once you have the 'Ah Ha' moment then go for it in a **Positive** manner.

You might wonder why I am discussing employment when you've discovered you have cancer. Well, if you are happily occupied then your work might be a welcome outlet where you are appreciated and you find a reason to go forward. I have observed that people who are happy in their occupations tend to live longer. Most of the great cartoonists lived long into their eighties and nineties. If you are unhappy about your job and can find a way to do it; cancer might provide a great excuse to re-evaluate how you spend your time and change your employment. Who knew that cancer could create an opportunity for you to exercise your freedom to quit or retire early?

They say the physical act of smiling will make you feel happier. Laughter is a positive mood lifter and it is something that every cancer patient should seek to do. I heard the story of a man who was given the news he had cancer and a short time to live. How did he handle the prognosis? He bought, borrowed or rented movies, all comedies and spent the next 6 months laughing his head off. When he went to see the doctor, he heard the happy news that his cancer was in remission. So laughter is the best medicine!

Researchers are studying the group of people called the Super Agers. This rare group of eighty to ninety year old senior citizens is remarkable for their exemplary aging. These active seniors are living long healthy lives and have brains and memory retaining abilities of people much younger than themselves. The Super Agers have more energy than others their age. Researchers have also discovered a common trait that the Super Agers share: that trait is a positive and inquisitive outlook. Research has linked that possessing a positive attitude helps your overall health. Isn't it amazing to think that being an optimist can help you to be healthier and grow old with all your wits about you?

Do you read the daily horoscope in the newspaper? You may think that advice based on your birthday is bogus. I sometimes read my horoscope because it gives me food for thought. I tend to take what I want from these words of guidance. One day my horoscope read: 'If you broadcast contented, satisfied, happy and energetic thought waves, you attract the best of everything.' What an endorsement for the power of being positive!

Cancer is a wakeup call – so no more waiting! Do what you want to do; you'll never have a better excuse for making a change. In having dealt with cancer, the fact that 'life is too short' has been hammered home to me. Cancer makes you realize that none of us are going to live forever. Live each day as though there is no tomorrow. Cancer has helped me to prioritize my projects and the goals I wish to accomplish before it is too late. I hope you will take my advice to heart.

CHAPTER 7

Why me?

We all ask that question when you are told you have cancer. For some people the answer is obvious. They might have made unhealthy choices such as smoking; drinking and using drugs and now realize their body is not impervious to poison and abuse.

Or you might have been exposed to cancer causing chemicals in your water, food or the environment and are now dealing with the consequences. And then there is the hereditary factor of cancer genes being passed down in your family. If you think you might have inherited cancer genes there are gene tests available. The BRCA and BART tests determine if you carry the breast cancer and/or ovarian cancer gene. Knowing if you carry the gene may help you in your decisions regarding various courses of treatment. The cost of doing these tests has been prohibitive; nine years ago my insurance carrier would not cover the BRCA 1, 2 and the BART. But recently the insurance industry has made some policy changes and my insurance company was willing to cover the tests. These test results are an important piece of information to share with family members so they can be aware of the risk of cancer running in your family. Knowledge is power. Your family members can be proactive and take steps to prevent cancer from occurring.

In my case, I was the last person anyone in my family would have thought would ever come down with Cancer. I was athletic and pretty much a goody, goody most of my life. Okay, maybe I over indulged in cocktails (weekends only) and when we enjoyed a cruise vacation I might have gained a few pounds. But I never did risky behavior that would have led me to believe that I would get cancer.

There was no family history of cancer that would have clued me in. My discovery of an egg sized lump in my right arm pit (swollen lymph nodes) that turned out to be cancer came out of nowhere. So, why me? Perhaps it is better for me to ask, why not me?

Dealing with cancer has given me a new appreciation for many, many things that in the past I might have taken for granted. For flowers to bloom there must be rain. I find now that I value a beautiful day like never before.

I also appreciate the power and beauty of storms and I find the physical experience of wind and lashing rain to be exhilarating. Friends, who are there for you or reach out to help, are deserving of a whole new level of appreciation, respect and love.

The dark edge of cancer in your life helps to define what is important. Think of a work of art, let's say a watercolor painting. If it is painted in soft pastel colors; well that might be pretty but also bland and a tad boring. If the painting has some darkness to it, a black line, a dark gray shadow, even a charcoal smudge that provides more definition: then the colors and highlights come into better focus and pop!

Try to think of your cancer experience as the shadow that helps to highlight the good elements of your life. A shadow gives a suggestion of depth to a painting and three dimensional qualities to sculpture. The shadow of cancer that will follow you forever, provides definition to your life. Cancer gives more depth and meaning to your existence and makes you realize how precious Life is.

Maybe some people live a sheltered existence where nothing bad or challenging ever happens to them. That kind of lifestyle sounds rather boring doesn't it? Cancer is a wakeup call. Without the contrast of happy to sad, sweet to sour, healthy to sick: your senses would not be stimulated to know the difference or sharpened to appreciate and recognize the better things in **Life!**

CHAPTER 8

Plan of Action

So you've gotten the news about your cancer condition. Now what do you do? Ask trusted friends for names of doctors and hospitals or medical facilities that they would be able to recommend. Be sure to check with your insurance company that these doctors are in their network of authorized providers. Whenever possible, get your insurance company's response in writing. It will save you hours of debate later on.

Interview the doctors as though they were auditioning for an important role with you – because they are! Make your decision based on the treatment described and the positive vibes you feel in working with the doctor and the associated medical team and facilities. Really listen to your inner feelings as you interview each prospective member of your cancer recovery team. Feeling good about working with a doctor that will help you to overcome and heal is extremely important to your well-being.

On the other hand, don't hesitate to fire a doctor if you don't gel. Your relationship is very important to improving your health. You need to find a good surgeon and ask for their recommendation for a great oncologist and plastic surgeon. Your doctor and team should have earned your trust in doing right by you and you should have confidence in their ability. Together you are working towards the goal of getting well. And a sense of humor is a plus in a doctor. I remember worrying about getting many more wrinkles from the chemo side effects i.e. the suppression of estrogen. My oncology doctor had a great sense of humor and replied, "That's good, we want you to have more wrinkles."

That statement gave me pause. More wrinkles? Well that means I'm aging, that I have a future to enjoy and wrinkles are the proof that I'm getting older 'which is a good thing', as Martha Stewart might say. It's hard to argue against the good will behind my doctor's sentiment!

CHAPTER 9

Tips, Nuts and Bolts of Cancer

I was in a groggy state of mind after my lumpectomy surgery when the surgeon greeted me with "you had cancer." I liked his using the past tense. I imagined that cancer was something in my past that it was dealt with and done. I had the surgery on a Friday and by the following Thursday I was on a plane. I didn't let cancer stop me from going to Malice Domestic, a cozy mystery writer's conference held in Washington D.C. I had been told not to lift anything heavy which was a problem. As usual, I had bought a fair number of signed hardcover books and had packed them into my carryon bag. I simply looked around for a strong looking guy, smiled and asked for his assistance in lifting my bag up into the overhead compartment. You see, my attitude has always been to not allow cancer to prevent me from reaching my goals. And if it means asking for a little assistance once in a while, that's okay; I will swallow my pride.

The Talk – have a thorough discussion with your doctor about the choices you have to make for your plan of treatment – to do a breast preserving lumpectomy with chemo and radiation or to do a mastectomy of the cancerous breast or a double mastectomy just to be done with it; these decisions have ramifications. Be sure to ask about the side effects of each procedure. Hindsight is always 20/20 and you will probably second guess your decisions. Get a second and third opinion or as many as you need to feel confident in going forward with the plan. You don't want to have regrets.

Lumpectomy – I chose this option to save as much of my breast as possible. The surgery resulted in my right breast being smaller than the left and it looked like a divot had been taken out such as you see on a golf course fairway. Years later I learned that the radiation of my right breast made it more difficult for my skin to stretch during breast reconstruction. In hindsight, perhaps I should not have been so married to my breasts… they were trying to kill me!

Bald – no big deal. I think having hair is way overrated. A month after starting chemo, my hair began to fall out. I tried to retain my hair but I noticed I was shedding pretty heavily and leaving little pieces of me wherever I went. So my husband, who had always helped to style and cut my hair, shaved my head. Without hair to shampoo and dry, getting ready in the morning was such a breeze!

It bummed me out when some of my eyebrows and eyelashes fell out but then I learned how helpful an eyebrow pencil, eye liner and mascara was for me to maintain a positive personal appearance. Since I'm a sporty gal I wore lots of different baseball caps which seemed to suit me just fine. Some ladies going through treatment don't bother with hats or make-up. More power to them!

Chemo – I handled it just fine. I was never sick. Sometimes I could taste a metallic flavor in my mouth and I did not taste flavors in quite the same way. Hence, the title of my book – 'To Know Sweet You Must Taste Sour'. I will share that I could taste and had a craving for mashed potatoes and clam chowder – go figure that one out. By the sixth and last chemo session I wondered what was wrong with me. I'd heard all the nightmare stories of people feeling sick and I'd not experienced any queasiness at all. In fact, I gained weight because a lot of people felt sorry for me and took me out to lunch. "Bring it on," I said and asked my oncologist to up the dosage on the final chemo treatment so I wouldn't have to go thru this again. I handled it like a poster child. For those people who find chemo makes them sick you have my sincere sympathy. Have faith in your doctor's chemo prescription and know that by enduring the treatment you are fighting the cancer and ridding your body of the disease.

Radiation – a snap. They form fitted a prop made of something like plaster used for a cast and then the doctor carefully mapped out the angles to radiate (**zap**) the right side of my chest – the tumor bed. I learned that I was lucky that the cancer hadn't been on my left side because it is trickier to radiate near the heart. They tattooed the roadmap for radiation and I had about eight sessions. I would put on a hospital gown, lie down on the prop that positioned me correctly and lifted up the right side of my chest. I closed my eyes so I wouldn't see the laser. They played nice relaxing music and I know I fell asleep at least one time. The office where this procedure was done offered pretty good cookies and coffee and I made a point of helping myself to it each visit. It's the little things like tasty cookies that can color a tedious medical treatment into a pleasant memory. I like to take advantage of the perks that come with cancer treatment. Ha!

Double Mastectomy – My oncologist suggested I consider doing this after a different form of breast cancer (estrogen positive) Stage 0 was discovered in my left breast. I interviewed a breast surgeon my oncologist recommended and agreed to the surgery. We discussed saving the nipples but since they were still breast tissue, to have kept them would have been risky.

I had my husband take a picture of me before/after just in case I ever wanted to do a sculpture of me. Bizarre… the thoughts that sometimes run through my head. The reality after all this breast reconstruction process is that when I look at myself, I think the plastic surgery has made me look better than I ever did. I'm much more youthful and perky now for a middle aged woman.

It is Important to Note: I had discussed various options before having the double mastectomy. Lumpectomy of my left breast, followed by chemo and radiation was an option. I chose to remove both breasts and thank goodness! My breast surgeon discovered some hidden tumors on the fringe of my left breast that were the sort of cancer tumors (estrogen positive) that left undiscovered could have spread all over. Whew! I recovered just fine, had the drain tubes removed and true to form just two weeks after surgery I was able to join friends on a gals trip!

Breast Reconstruction: I had to decide if I wanted to do this at the time of the double mastectomy operation. Why not try to make myself feel and look more normal? My insurance was covering the breast reconstruction so I thought it was a good thing to do. Implants were inserted and every week or so I went in to see the plastic surgeon for an expansion. I had hopes, my husband was even more hopeful that I might be able improve on what my bra size had been before but my skin was only able to give just so much. The right side had been radiated seven years before. What I didn't know at the time was that the flesh around my right breast would keep cooking for up to three years after the radiation. It was like trying to stretch treated leather and there was a concern if I tried for that DD, the implant might erupt due to tension stress. Who wants that to happen? I am very happy with my size today. Being the athlete that I am (golf, tennis, biking, kayaking, swimming etc.) bigger boobs would just get in the way.

Breast reconstruction can be a long tedious process. My plastic surgeon said giving my body time to stretch will help. Not everyone is patient and may opt not to bother with re-creating breasts. It's your choice. There will be scars and it may be a challenge to make your breasts a matched pair. To date it's been two years almost three since the second bout of breast cancer and I'm still doing some final tweaking. For me, I have no regrets.

Swapping out the expansion implants for more permanent ones was just a day surgery. I'm happy to say that I didn't let this surgery make me miss a beat. Two days post surgery I was able to attend my Master Naturalist class and enjoy sea kayaking with my fellow students. I was careful with my strokes and stayed in the middle of the group. I wouldn't have missed the experience of seeing tropical fish and sea turtles - it was a beautiful day!

Complete Hysterectomy: In consideration of my cancer history, I was advised to have my ovaries removed (Oophorectomy surgery). It's hard to believe they were still emitting estrogen but as long as I had my ovaries I was at risk for getting **Ovarian Cancer**. Since my ovaries were connected to my fallopian tubes which were connected to my uterus the discussion of the Oophorectomy progressed to suggesting a complete hysterectomy. It took me a while to come to terms with losing more of me; in this case the operation would be a preventive act. During a pelvic ultrasound a mass was detected in my cervix and quicker than you can blink I had the whole shebang removed by my gynecologic oncologist surgeon using the da Vinci Surgical System - (robotics) technique. I had the surgery on a Thursday and was able to join my walking group by Tuesday. My friends were amazed but have grown to expect me to be up and about in no time. The mass turned out to be nothing but served a good purpose to motivate me.

My message to you is to keep on going with your life and pursue your dreams.

Tips:

Go to a party – you know it's better to attend a wedding than to go to a funeral

Plan to participate in Relay For Life

Refuse to listen to scary cancer stories. Ignorance can be bliss.

Do something to help the Environment on our planet. Plant a tree. They say you grow flowers for your own enjoyment of the season but you plant a tree for the future generations!

Re-invent yourself! If you always wondered what it would be like to be blond – buy a blond wig. Fulfill your desires and fantasies.

Plan a Big Birthday party to celebrate your life and the friendships that have enriched it.

If you are feeling stressed out – let go and scream! Awful things sometimes happen but I will never let it get me down. I transfer the anger I feel into a positive energy. Find a way to turn the situation around. I will not let anything beat me. And because I'm a writer, I can always try to use the bad things that happen as material in a book. They say that writing is good therapy!

CHAPTER 10

Pain

Let me tell you about my pain experience. I haven't had to endure too much pain in my life so far. I recall one of the most painful episodes in my childhood was suffering with a terrible earache while up North at the family cabin. There were no hospitals or medical help nearby and everyone thought the earache would go away on its own. The pounding inside my head lasted for 2 days before subsiding.

The next memorable pain I recall was childbirth, the natural way without painkillers. That particular pain would build up, crest and then dissipate. Once I realized that pushing harder didn't make the pain any worse, I bore down and gave birth to my sons.

When I discovered the lump in my right armpit, I wondered if it was breast cancer. I did some internet research and read enough to scare me silly but I didn't share my concerns with anyone. I had ultrasound tests done and no one ever said a thing to confirm my worst fears. I went along with scheduling the surgery for getting a biopsy and kept my cool. I remained positive and did not share my worries with anyone. But fear is a strange thing. It causes stress that can manifest as nervousness, anger or in my case, pain.

I had just used the bathroom and as I stood up I was hit with a stabbing, excruciating pain in my lower back. I couldn't move without the painful agony spreading up or down my spine. I now have a profound new level of sympathy for chronic back pain sufferers. I cried out for help and my husband came and helped me to slowly stand. The pain gradually went away but now I was afraid that whatever I had that was causing lumps in my body had now spread to my back. I never spoke the words out loud but I feared that I had cancer in my spine. It turned out my husband who came to my rescue had the same fear but didn't share it with me. I tried not to think about it and kept myself busy until the surgery happened.

With my first surgery, I discussed strategy with my surgeon. The plan, if it turned out to be cancer was to do the lumpectomy followed by a series of chemotherapy treatments and then radiation. We decided that putting in a medical port would make getting the chemo much easier. I'd asked the surgeon to make the incision vertical so the scar would be hidden under my bathing suit strap but of course he made the incision horizontal. Maybe he had to make the cut that way; oh well; the scar is faintly visible when I wear tank tops. To me, the medical port felt like a bottle cap had been placed over my heart. Getting the chemo was no big deal; I never felt nausea – maybe just a metallic taste in my mouth and strangely enough a craving for mashed potatoes and clam chowder. The only pain I experienced was if I accidentally bumped or jarred the medical port.

Doctors and nurses control the pain you might feel after surgery and will probably give you a prescription for pain pills. Don't forget to ask your doctor or nurse important questions such as what is safe to take in addition to the pain pills. Or what to avoid taking (alcohol) while you are on pain medication. I was given oxycodone which worked just fine. A friend of mine warned me about the constipating effects of pain pills and gave me a yogurt based drink. Surgical drains are a pain, often catching on handles and tugging when you least expect it. But they do help with draining fluids away from the area on your body that experienced surgery. Make sure the nurse shows you how to milk the drains so you don't develop lymphedema. I handle pain pretty well and soon stopped taking the oxycodone.

However, I did make a painful mistake. After the total hysterectomy surgery that I underwent I was thirsty and grateful when soda pop was offered for the ride home. It didn't take long after I drank the pop for me to feel a pain in my stomach that grew in intensity. The carbon dioxide in the pop blew up inside me and I was in agony. The only solution was to walk it off and try to burp.

Don't stress the small stuff; or the big stuff! If you are in pain, consult with your doctor and they will help you to manage it safely.

CHAPTER II

Tennis and Golf

Growing up I had a few tennis lessons in school and a tennis PE class in college. I believe one of the reasons my husband and I clicked when we met is that I am athletic and enjoy being competitive. My husband helped me to improve my tennis game and this has become a lifelong source of companionship and fun exercise.

A typical day for us would be to get up early and play a round of tennis before starting to work. We enjoyed playing against each other or together as doubles partners so much that daily rounds of tennis was not unusual for us i.e. 7 days a week etc. I would hate to think what sort of shape I would be in today if I had not agreed to this exercise regimen. Not only has playing tennis helped me to keep fit but I have also had the pleasure of making new friends by playing in leagues and tournaments.

I have to credit this daily set of tennis with helping me to discover breast cancer before it spread further. Competitive exertion to win points equals sweat. And as a result of all that hard work I generally applied deodorant either before or after playing tennis. That's how I found the egg sized lump in my right arm pit - the swollen lymph nodes. My theory is that the strong muscles of my right shoulder kept the tumor suppressed until I exercised enough for the lump to pop out and present itself.

After surgery to remove the lymph nodes and the tumor in my right breast I was told to take it easy. My right arm felt tight like a rubber band was inside and stretched too taut. When I looked at the underside of my upper arm, it was dimpled in a straight line like a pulled thread in a piece of cloth. A few weeks after surgery I started to play some gentle tennis with my husband. For starters, I played up at the net. It wasn't long before I was bored with the net play and tried to serve a game. When I swung through on my serve (I'm right handed) I felt the pulled thread, rubber band tightness, give way. It didn't hurt and the amazing thing was that the line of dimples under my skin disappeared!

My tennis game gradually came back but I have to admit that my wicked serve lost some of its zip due to the surgery under my right arm and across my chest. Despite the difficulty with my serve, my husband and I have continued to enter the Cape Cod Community College educational fundraiser tennis tournament. This past summer the heat was debilitating and there was a strong wind factor that messed up many shots. I am absolutely thrilled to say that we prevailed and won our mixed doubles division! The following weekend, I was up against a tough opponent for my women's singles category. It was hot, humid and gusting winds would blow the ball out of the court. I used the same determination that got me through my cancer treatment to concentrate on winning, point by point. I left the tournament, a champion!

Our local tennis pros were all in awe of my determination to get back into the game and play competitive tennis again. In fact, a tennis pro who runs the Mixed Doubles Mixer that my husband and I like to play in Saturday mornings suggested I write about my experience. She thought my positive attitude was amazing and my words of encouragement and helpful advice might help others who are dealing with a similar experience. I tend to be a private person who does not open up and share but I gave serious thought about her suggestion. It would be one more way to turn a negative thing into a positive and I began to feel good vibes for this writing project. It is one of my personality traits to never let anything get the better of me. In other words; what doesn't kill me only makes me stronger. As a writer of mysteries I have always been able to vent and see justice served via fiction writing. Here was an opportunity to write creative non-fiction and be able to help others. Many thanks go to my tennis pro and all my friends for urging me to write about my experience in dealing with cancer.

My husband also loves to play golf. When I first met his family, I learned that his grandparents were avid golfers and they had played together all their married life. It impressed me that they were about to enjoy a 60th anniversary. It occurred to me that couples who played together, stayed together. So when my boyfriend, later husband offered to teach me how to play golf, I enthusiastically agreed.

Many pleasurable hours later, I had finally broken 100 when I found I had breast cancer. It took me a while to recover from the surgery but I was determined to not let cancer stop me from getting back into golf and improving my score.

I've heard conflicting advice about exercise after surgery. Some people say to take it easy because you don't want to overdo and cause lymphedema. The warning had something to do with the number of lymph nodes that had been removed from my right arm. Without those lymph nodes the circulation in my arm had been compromised. It's true that I did develop lymphedema swelling mostly in my upper right arm. Physical therapy involved stroking my arm and a compression device was prescribed for me. Wearing this hard case compression device at night was difficult. It felt like a club that I might accidentally hit my husband with during sleep. It was one of the few treatments that depressed me.

A friend who had been a nurse recited what she had advised former patients who were recovering from surgery; 'stretch for the stars and run your fingers up and down the wall'. It is important to follow the advice of physical therapists and be good about doing the rehabilitation work that they prescribe. Between the help I received from the physical therapist and my own efforts to exercise and get back to my usual routine, the swelling disappeared!

I love playing golf. I think it is one of the best ways to get outdoor exercise and at the same time spend hours in a beautiful landscaped environment. After my double mastectomy I tried to go slow and be careful that I didn't strain or tear anything. During my breast reconstruction process, silicone gel was injected. The goal was to be back to normal (whatever that is) and I hoped to improve and add to the breast size I was before cancer. Just so long as it didn't interfere with my golf swing, I joked with friends.

Now I am nearing the end of my breast reconstruction. My spirit was willing (to reach a full C) but my flesh was stronger and resisted stretching to that size. I had to accept what my body would allow and be satisfied with a full B which some friends say makes me appear more youthful than I really am. There's a tee shirt out there with a funny expression, 'I had a mastectomy to get rid of my breasts - they were trying to kill me!' That really puts it in the right perspective, doesn't it? I'm happy to say that I look athletically trim and fit and my new breasts don't interfere with my golf swing at all!

CHAPTER 12

The Power of Belief that you will get Well

When news of my cancer spread - my sweet worried husband just couldn't keep it to himself. I was touched by the outpouring of friendship and kind offers to help us ranging from driving me to doctor's appointments to making us meals. It was truly amazing!

You see, I might not have told anyone. It's not that I was trying to keep the cancer secret; it's just that I am naturally a quiet person who doesn't want to trouble anyone with my problems. Flowers from friends and relatives living at a distance brightened my days and lightened my heart. After my surgery, my amazing friends coordinated a delivery of food that was overwhelmingly generous. I cannot say Thank You enough!

I do not know how religious or spiritual you are but I found it heartwarming that many people wanted to include me in their daily prayers. Faith at a time like this can be a source of peace and strength to overcome adversity. All of these positive vibes surrounding me made me appreciate what a caring community I live in! My health issue opened my eyes to the positive connections we make on a daily basis with neighbors in your community when you volunteer. If you are not already actively volunteering in your hometown; get started immediately. Helping others truly helps you.

Many people commented on my positive attitude and wanted to know how I was able to handle everything so well and not get depressed. Well, I never gave cancer much thought. Just thinking about cancer gives it life and it had already intruded too much into my daily activities.

I was too busy making plans and writing and going along with the doctor's recommended course of treatment: lumpectomy surgery, chemo and radiation. I never contemplated anything not working out. By undergoing surgery I had rid my body of cancer. Now, I was doing what was necessary to prevent it from ever returning.

Beware of negative thoughts. They can get you down and attract bad luck. If you feel gloomy, give yourself a good shake and make a To Do list of activities you wish to accomplish. Reward yourself for being brave and following doctor's orders. I promised myself that after I was done with all the treatment, I would begin doing the things I always enjoyed such as art, writing, gardening etc. What are your wishes?

I attended some yoga classes and at the end while we relaxed, the teacher would have us envision ourselves surrounded by a white healing light. At this point in the yoga class I always concentrated hard on healing thoughts and being positive that all would be well. Do you believe in the power of mind over matter? Do you think your attitude can affect your health? Do you believe that a power within yourself which is open to interpretation (the Almighty) can be tapped into? I do!

Being positive, concentrating on good thoughts – becoming healthier and happy through quiet meditation, making wishes come true and finding peace in prayer; that is the right attitude to embrace. Believe me, you can make it happen!

CHAPTER 13

The Bucket List

What is on your Bucket List? From the Urban Dictionary comes this definition: A list of things to do before you die. This expression is also used when someone is dying as if he or she "kicked the bucket". I realized that I did not have a Bucket List unless my annual New Year's Resolutions counts as one. That was a sobering thought. I have too often made up New Year's Eve resolutions only to find at the end of the year, I had not accomplished them. In the past I might have thought, 'Oh well, there's always next year.' But now I had cancer. So I gave it some serious thought; if I were to die in a day, a week, a month, a year, five years... what would I like to accomplish with my time? What would I like to experience?

One interest I took up was to learn more about botanical art. I had always been fascinated by the ability of some artists to draw from nature so exactly that their illustrations could be used in scientific publications. So after I was finished with my final radiation treatment I enrolled in the Minnesota School of Botanical Art and started taking classes. I have travelled back and forth from Florida to Minnesota and so I still have two courses to take and then I must do a final project to complete my certificate. As Campfire Girls would say: Finish what you Begin - I am determined to accomplish my goal!

It is interesting to compare Bucket Lists with other people. My list contains many attainable goals and some that will be hard to reach. In the words of Benjamin Franklin, "Either write something worth reading or do something worth writing." I'm going for it!

Diane's Bucket List

1) Earn a Masters or Masters of Fine Arts degree
2) Visit Machu Pichu, Galapagos Islands & dance wildly in Kathmandu to 'Katmandu'
3) Attend the Masters Golf Tournament in Augusta, Georgia
4) Become a published author
5) Have a one-woman art show
6) Win a World Poker Tour event and a World Series of Poker bracelet
7) Attend all the Tennis Opens - worldwide
8) Participate in the Kentucky Oaks breast cancer activities & the Triple Crown
9) Win a championship at the Cape Cod Community College tennis tournament
10) Find a dog buddy and another cat pal
11) Finish editing my mystery novel and get it published
12) Finish editing my romantic suspense paranormal novel and get it published.

Your Bucket List

1)

2)

3)

4)

5)

6)

7)

8)

9)

10)

CHAPTER 14

Depression

If you feel down, say to yourself, "tomorrow is another, better day." Meanwhile, put a smile on your face and get busy with projects that have been put off or call a friend or go outside for a nice walk. To me, there is nothing that equals the peace I feel when I am outside enjoying a nature walk.

The time I remember feeling down during my second bout of cancer, was when the schedule for surgery was given and I realized that the operation was cutting it close to a planned trip with friends to New York City. It was childish I know but I cried, thinking I might not be able to go. But I never give up. I talked it over with my surgeons and found out that if all went well, if I rested as they advised and healed quickly… the drains would be removed and I could go as long as I did not lift my suitcase. I remained optimistic and thirteen days after surgery I was enjoying the Big Apple with my girlfriends!

A fellow Breast Cancer patient talked to me about her experience with depression. Her surgery and treatment had been similar to mine but I still had some procedures to complete. She warned me that after the last bit of work by the plastic surgeon had been done; I might experience depression the way she had. I thought about the effort that had been made to heal me and repair my body. The plan of action; treatment and plastic surgeries will soon be finished and I will have to live with the end result. Realizing that nothing more would be done, my breasts are as good as they're going to get, might be a disappointment.

I thought about what she said and had to consider it seriously. Was it possible that once the reconstruction process was done, once I was no longer being worked on and my body the center of much attention, I might become depressed? I realized that while you are being reconstructed there is hope that all will turn out well. Despite the plastic surgeon's best effort, once the job is done, reality might not meet your 'Great Expectations'. Slap yourself if you are disappointed. It's what's inside of you that really matters. Accept your appearance and be glad you are alive. It takes courage to get over disappointment and optimism to keep on living. The advice from Jim Valvano, former basketball coach and broadcaster should be kept in mind. "Don't give up. Don't ever give up."

So I plan to do what another Double Mastectomy patient did – once all the breast reconstruction work is done, I plan to go flash my surgeons. I hope everyone who sees me flashing, claps their hands in applause!

CHAPTER 15

Nature Walk

If things get to you and you're feeling down; go outside and enjoy a walk in the woods or go on a bike ride. It has been proven that experiencing Nature is good for your health. Enjoy it alone or call up a friend and take pleasure in some companionship. So many people will feel honored that you contacted them and will be pleased to be a companion on your path to wellness. So get outside to breathe some fresh air, don't sit around feeling sorry for yourself. Take advantage of a beautiful day to connect with nature.

Personally, I enjoy a quiet walk in the woods all by myself. Of course be careful, protect yourself and let people know where you are going. It gives me great peace to connect with Nature and experience the amazing environment of the world we live in. To listen to birds singing, insect orchestras throbbing away amongst the trees and hear the wind rustling through the tree leaves is a reminder that we are not alone in this world, merely a small part of it.

No one lives forever. At some point, we will all pass away and in some fashion or another return to the earth. It makes me content to know that in the circle of life, part of me will go on in some essential way unknown to me. I will return to Nature and I hope that my existence had an enriching impact on those around me.

CHAPTER 16

Loss of a Loved One

Just when you think you can't handle any more bad news, some other trouble happens. When it rains, it pours….. How many times have you heard that expression? Or trouble comes in threes? Our oldest child suffered a burst appendix (he recovered, thank goodness). My mother who was dealing with a painful back found out she had fractured some spine vertebra and was now facing the onset of osteoporosis. Then I was diagnosed with a return of breast cancer; you would think that I had suffered enough bad luck. But I was not going to get a reprieve.

I'd like to tell you about two special caregivers I have loved and who were there for me when I needed them most.

Matilda the Magnificent

After I was diagnosed with Breast Cancer, the first time around and had survived it, I knew the time had come to get another dog. You might ask why? I love animals and some of my best friends have been my pets. They say there is nothing like the unconditional love that a dog gives to you. I have been blessed with that experience and will be eternally grateful for being loved by my dogs.

So after my surgery and cancer treatment was done, I contacted my friend who is a dog breeder in Massachusetts. The time was right to get a puppy. I wanted a female bullmastiff because I had been told that females naturally bond with boys and she would become a good family guard dog. We named our beautiful fawn bullmastiff Matilda. It gave me a great sense of peace to think that if I didn't survive having breast cancer, our bullmastiff would still be there watching over and protecting my children. If we as a family trained her to be obedient and a good companion, Mattie would be a happy reminder to my sons of the good times we had shared.

TO KNOW SWEET YOU MUST TASTE SOUR

We purposely kept our backyard chemical free. Remember, I'd had cancer and had no desire to have anything to do with pesticides. It was a safe area for our new puppy to run around and for me to grow some herbs and vegetables. One evening we ran out into our backyard to play with Mattie. It was getting dark but we were having too nice a time to go back inside. An hour later as we walked into the house we saw our feet and legs were blue! Some sort of chemical dye was all over us and then we saw that it covered the grass in our backyard. One of my sons told me that he had noticed a pesticide worker near our house but when I called the company it was after hours and no one was there to respond to my outrage.

Not knowing what we had been exposed to; we showered and I washed the dye off Mattie's paws. It wasn't until the next day that my phone calls were answered. Management from the pesticide company came to our house and admitted that they had sprayed our yard without authorization. I told them I felt like they had committed a chemical attack on me and my family. They reassured me that the pesticide was totally harmless; its composition was made up of chrysanthemums. I did not believe the pesticide executives but there wasn't any evidence that I could dig up at that time to prove them wrong. Our doctor wasn't concerned and so I let it go… until it all came back to haunt me three years later.

In that time, Matilda had grown up to be a beautiful show quality blue ribbon winner. She had also become my best friend and a great loving companion to my husband and the boys. Mattie had fulfilled my expectations and would be a wonderful guardian for my family for years to come. To this day, I still tear up when I think about what happened to her.

In late spring, I noticed that Mattie was reluctant to trot around the dog show ring. It was a beastly hot summer and I thought the humidity and high temperature outside was getting to her. Mattie had gotten some infection earlier in the spring which the vet prescribed antibiotics for her. She never complained but continued to act lethargic in the heat.

Later on that summer I brought her back to the vet and we were hit with the tragic news that our beloved Mattie was suffering from renal failure. The vet asked if there was a family history of kidney disease or if she had gotten into antifreeze. I was insulted at the questions - as though I would let my valuable dog run loose. I checked with my friend, a very reputable breeder who had sold Matilda to us and she confirmed what I already knew: no history of kidney disease. For weeks I dosed Matilda with medicine and fluids and prayed for her to heal.

My youngest son brought his girlfriend over so she could say goodbye. In the past Matilda had viewed this girlfriend as competition for her boy and had tested this young woman's determination to stay with my son. Mattie was resting outside in the shade when they approached and my son said, "Mattie, look who's here to see you."

I will never forget how Mattie struggled to rise, her tail thumping against the ground in happy greeting at seeing the girlfriend with my son, as though saying "Oh beloved enemy! We may have competed before for my boy's attention but I am so glad you are here. Please look after him for me."

We tried to save her but to no avail… we had to put Mattie to sleep. I believe our dog died of kidney failure that was caused by pesticide exposure when she was a puppy. During the time she was with us, Mattie was a wonderful, loving caregiver. To this day we feel robbed; needlessly deprived of years of her companionship and love… a tragedy caused by pesticide poison.

Yoda, our cat

I have shown that I am tough and can handle the lemons that life throws. The straw that broke the camel's back was bringing our beloved cat, Yoda to the veterinarian for a checkup when we noticed he had lost his appetite. Several examinations, tests and x-rays later we were told he had incurable cancer. It was too much. My husband and I cried far more over his situation than my own.

He was never a lap cat. Yoda preferred to drape himself across the tops of sofas. He sported a perpetual smile and always looked incredibly relaxed. Yoda exuded peace and contentment. His message to us was 'chill, all will be well'. His purr was the loudest I have known. Yoda was a lover not a fighter; but definitely he was the "Dude" in our home.

When I learned that Breast Cancer had returned for a second time, my family and friends were amazed at how well I handled everything. It's true, I possess a stoic optimism but I will admit I had trouble with sleeplessness. At night, while lying awake, thinking about some heartache I was feeling in addition to the cancer… my hidden despair was felt by one of my caregivers: Yoda. Somehow he knew I was feeling troubled and sad. More than once, Yoda would surprise me when late at night he would jump up on the bed and purr loudly as he tried to comfort me. And it worked! I would relax and fall asleep listening to that comforting purr.

Imagine our heartbreak when just a few months later, Yoda's appetite disappeared and the veterinarian's prognosis was incurable cancer throughout his stomach. I was now the caregiver and determined to save him… all for naught. Our best efforts were not enough, he wasn't eating and the meds did nothing. When Yoda stopped purring – we knew it was the end.

What do you do when life is unfair? Certainly you give yourself time to grieve and recover. Give yourself some space to deal with your emotions. There's an expression, 'Time heals'. Try to think that tomorrow will be a better day, even if you doubt it; say it in a positive manner. Go for a walk in the woods and appreciate the beauty of nature. Time does heal and the pain of the loss of a loved one will ease. Try to remember the good times you shared and treasure those positive memories.

There is nothing like a great pet. Their devotion and sensitivity to your moods is amazing. Isn't it odd how sometimes it is easier to express your feelings of love to a pet than to people? Pets ask for nothing more than food, shelter and companionship and in return give unconditional love. After hearing what happened, some people suggested that maybe Yoda somehow took the cancer I was fighting into his body as a final act of love. Who knows?

If there is any good to come out of the well of misery you might find yourself in: it is to realize that Life is too short. So hug those you love and tell them how much they mean to you. Never take for granted that there is a better time to express your feelings. Say you love them, **Now**! Each day could be the last; so live each moment to the fullest!

CHAPTER 17

Strength and Humor

My strength and sense of humor; friends have asked me, where does it come from? The answer is: my grandmothers and my parents. Both of my grandmothers were terribly important to me and gave me great happiness when I was a child. Your relatives can give you great encouragement and characteristics they possess can give you a model to copy.

I can attribute my strength to my Scandinavian mother. She always thought of herself as stoic. The meaning of stoic is; someone who can endure pain or hardship without showing their feelings or complaining. My Mom has always shown great fortitude when facing troubles that would bring most people to their knees. Even on the coldest day in winter, when asked about the weather she would reply that it's beautiful. I knew that I would never get an accurate portrayal of the weather Up North because no matter how much it snowed or how brutally cold it might be; to my mother there is a beauty in the cold winter. It's just a matter of adopting the right attitude. I was inspired by Mom to handle the medical treatments in a novel way. I would not let getting chemo treatments restrict my mobility. Once I had the medical port put in: I felt free to travel. After all, the chemo cocktail my oncologist prescribed for me was a recipe that other doctors and nurses could copy. It's not like they would keep it a secret from each other. My attitude was; have medical port; will travel! I had chemo doses given to me in Orlando, Minneapolis and Cape Cod. Mom was worried about me and just clueless about cancer. She showed her concern and love by keeping me company during my Minnesota chemo treatments. To this day, she's perplexed about why I ever got cancer. She always thought of me as being the most athletic and the healthiest of her children. I have the dubious honor of being the first person in my family to be diagnosed with cancer. To my mother's knowledge, cancer did not run in her family. So she blamed the cancer as coming from my Dad's side of the family tree. Ha ha ha!

Just thinking about my father brings a smile to my face. He was the life of the party, a happy go lucky Scotch Irishman with a great fondness and talent for telling jokes and stories. I knew I favored his side of the family because every now and then he'd look at me and say how much I reminded him of his mother. My father was a medal winning sprinter in school and knew how to fight. He was a Marine Sergeant in WWII, trained in the Mojave Desert, served in the Pacific and boxed during the war.

During his life, my father faced much adversity; being poor, growing up in a single breadwinner household, surviving WWII and working hard for a living as a bartender. All my life I watched my dad handle problems head on and roll with the punches. No matter how badly some people might have treated him, my father maintained a sunny upbeat attitude. That's why my mother fell in love with him; he made her laugh.

At my father's well attended funeral, I found out from several of his acquaintants and friends just how much he had helped people by telling jokes and being a good listener. At the end of a bad day, my dad was there to make light of your problems and put a smile on your face. He had a gift for humor and we all miss him deeply.

They say laughter is the best medicine. Keep that in mind as you deal with cancer. There is no reason to endlessly worry over things you can't change. We should all aspire to be stoic which is being able to carry on under a burden. Follow the advice of your medical professionals and do not entertain negative thoughts. A positive attitude can work wonders!

CHAPTER 18

How Cancer made me a better Poker Player

I love to play games and have recently learned to play Mah Jong and Bridge. But the card game I have grown to love most of all is Texas Holdem Poker. During some down time after surgery I discovered while flipping channels on the TV, the World Poker Tour and the World Series of Poker. I found it captivating to watch the strategy various players used and listening to the commentators took my mind off my health issues. This variation of poker has become wildly popular around the world with huge tournament jackpots offered and won by those card players who know how to play the odds, are willing to learn strategy and be aggressive.

I have found there are many similarities between dealing with cancer and playing the cards dealt to you in poker. So I have come up with some analogies comparing poker terms and how it relates to handling cancer. I'm not saying gamble with your life; take your doctor's advice for treatment seriously and do everything you can to increase the odds in your favor. However, life is a gamble so go out there and have some fun!

Playing the Hand dealt to you. In Texas Holdem Poker each player is dealt two cards and betting may occur thereafter. *With Cancer, this is when the Doctor breaks the news to you about your health and you devise a plan of treatment.*

Expected Value Bet – a long term effect of making certain decisions. *What health choices, both diet and exercise have I made or that I can still make that will change the outcome?*

Ante – everyone contributes a small bet the longer you play in a tournament. *That might be considered your monthly Healthcare payments.*

Five community cards are dealt that you can play off to mix with and to improve the two cards originally dealt to you. You can check or bet in between the third, fourth and fifth card. *Your community cards are there to help you – neighbors, friends, family and your hospital and medical advisors.*

Flop – is the first three cards
Turn – the fourth
River – the fifth and last card to make or improve your hand
Bad Beat – An unexpected losing hand when you had strong odds of winning. *This would be a setback in your treatment. The courage to play on shown by cancer patients is inspiring, quite frankly - truly amazing!*

The Nuts – is the best possible hand in the game – at that particular moment. This situation can change as you go along but it certainly affects how you play your cards. *In Cancer – this is a good prognosis!*

Drawing Dead – To be in a position where there is no chance to improve your hand against an opponent. *Well, bad news is bad news. This is the time to wear your best poker face and put your affairs in order.*

Bluffing – In poker, this is making a bet and acting as if you have the best hand when in fact you have been dealt lousy cards. You hope to win the hand with aggressive betting and making your opponents believe you have a better hand than you actually have. *With Cancer patients this is the* brave face we show the world. Hope springs eternal and miracles do happen!

All In – The Push literally shoving all your chips into the pot. This Live or Die action to win the pot puts your future into the hands of Fate. *Relating to Cancer – this is having Faith!*

Final Table – in a tournament, this is where you have been fighting to reach! *For Cancer survivors this is the last bout of chemotherapy or radiation. What we have learned is it's important to apply your best effort to play the game and hope for winning results!*

My final thoughts on playing games are that it's a good way to escape for a little while from reality. It's been proven that playing games stimulates your brain and helps you to stay sharp as you get older. And we all know that getting older is winning the jackpot!

CHAPTER 19

Tempting Fate

I missed a mammogram appointment when I was forty years old because we were moving out of state. I never rescheduled the mammogram and years passed by without my being proactive about my health. Mammograms are a preventive examination that might catch breast cancer in the early stages. Do as I say, not as I did! A kick in the pants will hit you when you least expect it. That's what happened to me while I was working on this book. Here's a quick review: in 2004 I went thru Breast Cancer treatment in my right breast. I was advised to do a lumpectomy followed by chemotherapy and then radiation. I followed the doctor's orders and trusted their expertise. Tempting fate and doing nothing is not an alternative.

For years I did not know what type of Breast Cancer I had (please note the use of the past tense). I was told after three years that I was out of the woods. After five years had passed, people told me I was golden. A Tuesday Walkers friend going through treatment asked me what kind of Breast Cancer I had and I found out that the breast cancer I had dealt with years earlier was just like hers, an aggressive type – Triple Negative.

Well now I was at seven and a half years, cancer free and I felt I could heave a sigh of relief, sit back, think beautiful thoughts and. . . Not so fast, Diane. During my annual mammogram, a doctor spotted what looked like a tiny broken string of pearls in my left breast. A biopsy revealed that I had another form of Breast Cancer, this time it was estrogen positive. So I had the operation for a double mastectomy with breast reconstruction. During a visit with my oncologist, the bug was put in my ear that I might want to consider having my ovaries removed. The argument put to me was that my ovaries weren't doing me any good (at age fifty-four I wasn't planning on having more children) and those ovaries might still be sending out estrogen. So why take a chance on continuing to feed cancer? I had some time to think about it but I would need to make a decision before the end of the year. Some residual vanity I possessed made me want to cling to some estrogen so I wouldn't age and wrinkle prematurely. Someone said that the removal of my ovaries would be a life altering decision that would push me into menopause with all the side effects; vaginal dryness being one of them. So I took my time and put off the decision.

Following the double mastectomy surgery I made several visits over the next 6 months to the plastic surgeon for implant expansion and eventually when my radiated flesh would stretch no more, I swapped out the temporary implants for more permanent ones. Never one to lie around recovering, a couple of days after surgery I was sea kayaking with my Coastal Studies class, the first leg in my pursuit of a Master Naturalist certificate. I'm sure the plastic surgeon would not have approved but I did not want to miss out on the fun. I did exercise with caution while I kayaked with my class on the Atlantic Intracoastal Waterway of Florida. I was careful, slow and gentle with the movement of my strokes and I thoroughly enjoyed the field trip and did not hurt myself in the process.

After a summer spent recovering and visiting with relatives, I returned to more doctor visits and some genetic counseling. I hoped that my insurance company would cover the cost of doing a BRAC 1, 2 and the BART test. It would be an extremely helpful bit of information in deciding what surgery to do – none or just the ovaries or a complete hysterectomy. I learned that because of the chemotherapy I had taken 8 years ago, I was already into menopause. Silly me, I'd already been dealing with the life altering side effects. A new study came out that indicates that if you had Triple Negative Breast Cancer, as I did 8 years ago, then my chances are very high that I will get Ovarian Cancer. It seemed prudent for me to agree to the complete hysterectomy.

Just when you think things can't get worse… the other shoe drops. I went and got a pelvic ultrasound and guess what? A mass was discovered in my cervix and so I had to go in to see the gynecologist/oncologist surgeon for a biopsy. The biopsy report came back as negative for cancer but after that scare, I didn't hesitate to schedule the complete hysterectomy. It was like; how fast can it be done?

As usual, I kept myself busy with various projects and community activities. I managed to remain calm and to be positive about the upcoming scheduled surgery. They say that **Stress** is a contributing factor to getting Cancer. Sometimes I find it is a struggle to not lose my temper. So I have learned to take several deep breaths, grab my journal and write down my thoughts before I waste energy blowing up.

In retrospect I am glad that I went ahead with all of these surgeries. Side effects that were a concern such as vaginal dryness can be dealt with using lubricants. Wrinkles can be kept at bay with moisturizers and staying out of the sun. And so with a positive attitude that all will turn out right - I fight on!

Nothing will get me down. I'm still here and my friends say I'm looking better than ever!

CHAPTER 20

Seven Stages of Grief as it relates to Cancer

Friends asked me if I had experienced the Seven Stages of Grief when I learned I had cancer. They thought I might be stuck on denial since I had handled everything so well. I looked up this Seven Stage concept and learned that it relates to how you feel during a break up of a relationship. If you think of your good health as the relationship you have with your body it is interesting to make comparisons.

This is my interpretation of the Seven Stages of Grief as it relates to Cancer.

Shock or Disbelief – Discovering that you have Cancer can be a nasty surprise that is hard to believe. I was dumbfounded by the news. I considered myself to be a pretty healthy person with never a broken bone and I'd never been in a hospital other than to give birth to my three boys. Cancer did not run in my family.

Denial - I never felt sick in a way that I imagined you would if you had a deadly disease. It crossed my mind from time to time that maybe someone had made a mistake about the lump in my arm pit. That the swollen lymph gland was a bad reaction to a cold I'd been fighting. Fortunately I continued to meet with doctors to figure out what was wrong.

Anger – When I learned I was fighting breast cancer I looked into the question of; why me? Environmental exposure to carcinogens and stress are thought to cause cancer. I thought about the old creosote plant that was rumored to have leaked into the drinking water of the town I grew up in. If stress causes cancer, I had experienced enough arguments and stressful situations in my life that might explain why I was made vulnerable to getting cancer. It makes me mad to realize that I am a victim to environmental human generated poison.

Bargaining – With cancer, bargaining might be the deals we make with ourselves to resolve to eat better and make healthy choices. It might involve making a bargain with God i.e. 'if I behave better, please help me get well' etc.

Guilt – Questions come to mind. Did I get cancer because I was overindulgent? Guilty as charged. If I had avoided certain stressful situations – leave the room, turn the other cheek or simply avoid the source of stress instead of experiencing confrontations… would I be cancer free? I don't think it is wrong to stand up for yourself but is there a way I could have avoided stress? When I get upset I can't sleep. More and more research seems to indicate that lack of sleep is the cause of all sorts of health problems such as cancer and obesity. Someday doctors will know the answers to these problems but getting a good night's sleep is increasingly important.

Depression – Well it's very easy to feel sorry for yourself when you have cancer. Giving in to negative thoughts will only make you feel hopeless. Use the tips I have written about and climb out of the well of misery. Go out and volunteer for the many organizations in need of help and you will feel needed and therefore better.

Acceptance – The relationship you had with your body and general health has been shaken up with having cancer. Now that you have followed your doctor's advice, gone through treatment and are recovering it is time to build a better relationship with your body and strive for good health.

CHAPTER 21

Losing Weight

As I have said before, I chose not to spend much time studying up on cancer. I feel that dealing with cancer has already taken up enough of my time and I have no interest in becoming an expert on cancer. That being said, I do know others and have friends who have become authorities on the subject. I do not have a problem with listening to their advice on the latest cancer research or suggestions for treatments.

Several of my friends attended a symposium that informed them about all the variables that play on your chances of getting cancer that you might have no control over. But there is one thing that you can do that does have an impact on your cancer prognosis – it is Lose Weight!

You may not be able to alter your genes if you have inherited the cancer gene or have suffered environmental exposure to carcinogens but you can control your weight. Some people say that fat nourishes cancer or that cancer hides in fat: so why provide cancer with a friendly environment for it to thrive in?

Three years ago I decided to lose weight once and for all. After consulting with my oncologist, I made a very serious effort at it. I ate less and exercised more. My husband and I split meals and in addition to our morning tennis session we added an evening round of tennis playing. I drank lots of water and tried to walk and ride my bike more, drive the car less. I made great progress and looked fabulous!

Becoming thinner also saved my life! With less fat to see through, the mammogram doctor at the hospital spotted the dots of cancer that looked like a tiny broken string of pearls. **Thank you!** By slimming down I helped myself in so many ways. I'm still working at keeping the weight off. Losing weight and exercising more is a lifestyle change that can truly be of help to you.

Lose weight under your doctor's care and guidance. This is a lifesaver of a decision on your behalf. Go for it! Just think; if you are overweight you may have plenty to lose but you will have every health benefit to gain!

CHAPTER 22

Healthy Choices

At a recent Garden Club meeting I attended I learned more about the terrific health benefits to Juicing and making Smoothies! The speaker gave us numerous tips about the healthy aspects of blending fruits and vegetables and shared her favorite recipes. I am thinking there is something to be said about using blender drinks to help us all eat healthier. Remember the old saying; you are what you eat? In addition to planning to add a blended juice drink to my own intake of vitamins, I realize that making up a healthy drink for a loved one who is dealing with cancer might be beneficial in multiple ways. The speaker pointed out that the Juicing pioneers are living longer and most importantly are active and healthy seniors. Here are a few notes I took.

Any blender will do for making smoothie drinks.

Your lifestyle affects your health. Listen to your body, detect early and do something about it. Your body is always trying to heal itself and if you add Juicing to your lifestyle, you give your body a fighting chance. Exercise will also help you to fight cancer.

Eat the rainbow of colors when juicing.

Fresh is usually better but Frozen fruit was picked at its peak and is convenient.

Blend up apples and carrots to fight cancer. For juicing carrots you can use pureed baby food.

Whole pears and apples best are for fiber. Watch your intake of bananas unless you want to gain weight.

Local wildflower honey is great for allergies.

Avocado has good fat.

Pomegranate is good for your heart.

Consider alternative products to regular cow milk which may contain chemicals, growth hormones & antibiotics. Consider using almond milk, coconut milk, soy milk or flaxseed milk.

Juicing – drink right away, good for 24 hours, after that the good enzymes are gone but you still get your veggie allowance.

Blending – Great for picking up pounds if you or someone you are caring for is underweight. Keep in mind that Fiber and Water slow down the blood sugar absorption.

TO KNOW SWEET YOU MUST TASTE SOUR

A friend pointed out that vegetables and the fiber you ingest should be given preference over fruit juices. According to Kim Kirschner, "smoothies provide the same benefits as juicing plus fiber, which helps the body, rid itself of toxins, excess hormones and cholesterol and promotes healthy gut activity."

Please remember you should do everything in moderation. If you have any questions about what to blend and if it will work with your medication, please consult with your doctors. So put this advice and good thoughts into action and consider adding a smoothie drink into your weekly meal plans.

CHAPTER 23

Journaling

While you are dealing with your health challenge you might find writing in a journal to be a great help. This journal can be as simple as a spiral bound notebook and/or you can upgrade to a more expensive leather bound blank book. Pick whatever inspires you.

In the past, keeping a diary was common practice with people writing just a passage or a few pages in their diary or journal on a daily basis. Some of these diaries might have been a simple record of the weather. On the other hand, diaries may have been much more personal serving as a place for the writer to pour out their heart. In either case, diaries have often added historical detail to past lives;

have been fascinating to read because they provide insights into the lives of the diarists.

Writing in a journal is a quiet activity that may give you a few moments of peace. Putting pen to paper and writing about your experience is a meaningful way to share with your family what you are going through. This is a great opportunity to convey your nuggets of wisdom and reflect upon your life as lived up to this point. What have you learned? What is important for you to express? Writing can be a cathartic exercise. If you are stressed, you can vent in your journal and release the negative energy. You're only human – it's alright to express any frustration in your journal and hopefully feel a sense of relief. I find the best time for me to write in my journal is at the end of the day.

Keeping a Health Journal helps you to log your treatment and mark your progress to getting well. Write questions that come to mind in your journal. If you can't manage to do the writing during your appointment, have someone such as a caregiver write the answers to your questions in the journal. Being able to refer to these notes is amazingly helpful when discussing your worries and concerns with your doctors. Keeping track of one important notebook or journal helps when you are in a hurry to get to a doctor's appointment.

In addition to my notebook I also have a designated cloth shoulder bag to hold the journal, pens and miscellaneous medical paperwork that accumulates as you progress along with your healthcare treatments and operations. A colorful bag makes it easier to find. There is a saying that goes something like: 'you think you can leave your troubles behind but you carry them with you wherever you go.' At least with my suggestion you can be better organized for your important medical appointments.

Journal Thoughts

CHAPTER 24

The Power of Faith

In this chapter I want to talk about faith. Whatever your religious orientation, when you are given the message that you have cancer, it might really throw you for a loop. Atheists become religious church goers and religious people who have led good lives feel cheated or tricked and might lose faith.

I would hope that you might give yourself time to absorb the news and don't act or react in a hasty manner. I don't have an answer as to why good people, young and old are hit with cancer. Prayer is helpful and can bring you peace. Reaching out to have a private conversation with God can begin a discourse and/or argument that can assist you with understanding and accepting your condition.

If you are reading my book because your child has cancer… it must seem that Fate and/or God is being extremely unfair. Some people will express platitudes such as God wants your baby as an angel or that only the good die young. Those sayings may put some balm on your pain but it also might trigger a rage at the horrible situation you are dealing with.

Talking to a minister or religious counselor might help. I suggest that in addition, you might find that reading from the Bible, the Koran or whatever religious writings are in existence that you find appealing might bring understanding, acceptance and peace to you.

My sympathies and condolences go out to those of us dealing with cancer… Remember, you are not alone; having Faith can help you cope.

CHAPTER 25

Putting your Affairs in Order

If you have not already done so, now is the time to write out your will. A Last Will and Testament is a legal document for your estate that bequeaths your valuables and assets. There are estate planners who can help you to decide what is best for you and your family. I attended a class on estate planning and was very impressed with the Revocable Living Will Trust. In essence, this legal document allows you to establish how you want to leave your assets to whom, how much, etc. In addition, there are funds to draw on to take care of your medical needs should you be incapable of keeping in control and on top of your affairs. All of this is drawn up as you wish, not what some probate official disperses.

There is a Health Directive that leaves instructions for your family members or friends to follow that can relieve them of making those decisions for you. Why burden your relatives with hard to make decisions when they are in the grip of strong emotions? Make your wishes known.

A new trend is creating an Ethical Will. This Will might be a letter filled with words of helpful advice; it can describe your life experience and reflect your personal values. This is a great opportunity to share favorite memories and family traditions, to reflect on choices you made that impacted the life you have lived. Ethical wills can consist of photos, art you created, scrap books, family recipes and favorite music. Sharing with loved ones what you valued most, your attitudes that shaped your character and career is a great way to come to grips with your own mortality and leave a legacy of wisdom that would be treasured by future generations.

Be proactive and plan your funeral! Believe it or not; this can be fun and will take a load of difficult choices off your family or trusted friend's shoulders. This can be treated in an entertaining fashion. What music do you like? Are there photos or videos that you want to have running in the background? When my father died it fell to me to gather up photos of his life and bring them to a company that specializes in funeral videos. I think I did a pretty good job but I know after that experience that I would like to create my own and really personalize my farewell message.

What is your legacy?

CHAPTER 26

Cancer Events

Participation in cancer events can be very gratifying. Often your hospital will make you aware of various cancer patient groups that gather weekly in one of their meeting rooms. Discussions are led under the guidance of health professionals. In a cancer support group, you will find answers to your questions and be able to address your fears in a friendly atmosphere.

I have gone to breast cancer support group meetings at two different Florida Hospitals and found it helpful but not something I wanted to make a weekly or monthly habit of attendance. You might want or need the caring and concerned camaraderie of fellow cancer patients and that's great. Every individual who finds they are facing a health challenge such as cancer has the right to deal with it in their own way. However, I wouldn't advise you to keep your cancer prognosis to yourself. Misery loves company and it feels good to vent once in a while and you might learn something new from another person's cancer experience. Just remember that there are many various groups and organizations out there willing to lend an ear and/or give you a group hug should you need it.

There are sure to be several cancer events where you live. These day or weekend long events can be a lot of fun. I saw one such event on Cape Cod that was a fishing competition and another was a walk, swim and bike activity. I had plans that conflicted with being able to participate but I hope to next year. One thing you learn as you are dealing with cancer; on this journey you never walk alone. There are many people in the same boat and joining together to make a positive difference has a wonderful healing effect. So, go ahead and participate!

I have participated in Relay For Life, both as a fundraiser for cancer research in remembrance of friends I've lost and as a Survivor participant. I was very proud and honored to be asked to be the keynote speaker one year. I've been amazed at the commitment some people show at Relay For Life and wondered if some of them are wrestling with feelings of regret. Did they not spend enough time with the person they lost? Are they sad and in an effort to cope they want to raise research money to eradicate cancer? Many of the volunteer participants have never had cancer and yet here they are spending the night walking to raise money for cancer research. Lighting a luminary dedicated to someone who is fighting cancer and/or walking all night in honor of a loved one they lost to cancer can be a part of the healing process. I imagine there are a variety of motivations and they are all good if the end result is a shared determination to put an end to this disease.

My theory that to know sweet, you must taste sour applies here. The death of a friend or relative to cancer helps you to appreciate your remaining friends and family all the more. Don't be silent about your feelings for others. Have the pleasure of expressing your affection and love and make happy memories while you can.

I recently walked in a Pink on Parade fundraising event that was amazing for the sense of camaraderie and community involvement. Participating in a walk with other people who care about beating cancer reminds you, once again, that you do not walk alone.

CHAPTER 27

My Favorite Books

Another way to take your mind off the drudgery and depression of fighting cancer is to escape into another world by re-reading a favorite book or discovering a new writer and their work. I would like to share with you some old friends from my childhood that I suggest for you to read and new discoveries that got me through tough times.

1) The Hobbit and the Lord of the Rings series by JRR Tolkien
2) The Song of Ice and Fire series, A Game of Thrones etc. by George R R. Martin
3) My Friend Flicka, Thunderhead, Green Grass of Wyoming by Mary O'Hara

4) And then there were None and many more by Agatha Christie
5) Harry Potter series by J K Rowling
6) The Thin Woman by Dorothy Cannell
7) Crocodile on the Sandbank by Elizabeth Peters
8) The Sweetness at the Bottom of the Pie series by Alan Bradley
9) Tom Sawyer by Mark Twain
10) Black Beauty by Anna Sewell
11) Wicked Plants, Wicked Bugs by Amy Stewart
12) The Name of the Wind, The Wise Man's Fear by Patrick Rothfuss
13) Conan the Barbarian by Robert E. Howard
14) Anne of Green Gables, series by Lucy Maud Montgomery
15) Nancy of Paradise Cottage by Shirley Watkins
16) Little Women, Little Men by Louisa May Alcott
17) Sherlock Holmes by Sir Arthur Conan Doyle
18) Romance novels by various authors; Laura Kinsale, Madeline Hunter, Christina Dodd, Lisa Kleypas.
19) Any Travis McGee novel by John MacDonald
20) Any Jack Reacher novel by Lee Child
21) Gone with the Wind by Margaret Mitchell
22) World War Z by Max Brooks

CHAPTER 28

My Favorite Movies

Choose to watch old favorites; it's like spending an afternoon with a close friend. Be open to new movies coming out that will take you out of your world and into another place at least for a few hours. My suggestion; pick movies that will make you laugh! I heard a story about a guy who found out he had terminal cancer. He rented a bunch of comedies and laughed himself into remission. They say that laughter is the best medicine!

1) The Bank Dick
2) Mrs. Doubtfire
3) Laurel and Hardy films
4) The Marx Brothers films

5) Caddy Shack
6) 1941
7) The Birdcage
8) Ace Ventura, The Mask, Dumb & Dumber, Liar, Liar - any Jim Carrey comedy
9) The Thin Man series with Myrna Loy and William Powell
10) On the Road films with Bob Hope and Bing Crosby
11) North by Northwest
12) Casablanca
13) Wuthering Heights
14) Overboard
15) The Wizard of Oz
16) Murder by Death
17) Abbott and Costello meets Frankenstein
18) Jaws
19) Scent of a Woman
20) It's a Wonderful Life
21) The Hobbit and Lord of the Rings series of films

CHAPTER 29

Bottle of Optimism Email

This is an email letter from the fall of 2011 that I wrote to friends and family informing them that Cancer had returned. This was hard to do because I don't like to talk about my health – it's an uncomfortable subject that I don't want to bring attention to normally. I tried my best to keep this email light hearted and upbeat. Here is how I described what I was going through.

Subject: Breast Cancer - Again

Dear Friends,

I am sorry to be writing my news as an email but... it's hard to sometimes talk about my health (the phone battery runs out) or next to impossible to run into everyone and be able to tell you personally so here's the news. A routine mammogram in late September, biopsy in early October, detected Breast Cancer at Stage 0 (ductal carcinoma in situ) had returned but this time to my left breast. Hey - I thought breast feeding my sons (22 - 28 years ago) was supposed to help prevent this? HA! Anyways, this cancer is seen as a separate event from the breast cancer (triple negative) that I dealt with 7 years ago. So my oncologist has recommended by-lateral mastectomy with two-part breast reconstruction to follow. Several second opinions have confirmed that in my case: this is the best manner of dealing with it.

So this next Tuesday November 15th I will be at Florida Hospital South (Walt Disney Cancer Institute) having surgery. Believe me this is no Mickey Mouse operation! I met with an Italian Plastic Surgeon and asked if my breasts would be in good hands - was he an artist? Better yet: how skilled was he at sculpting? He is the Chairman of Plastic Surgery for Florida Hospital so he must be good - anyways... only Chris will ever know how well it turned out. The surgeon is a lady doctor who specializes in Breast Surgery and they often work as a team. So I think I am in good hands!

Well you know what they say... When life serves you lemons... I intend to turn them into grapefruits! As long as the new boobs don't interfere with my tennis game or golf swing, I'll be OK!

This will give me a great opportunity during my convalescence to catch up on reading, writing and doing botanical art! Chris is just wonderful and will take good care of me. I am blessed to have such a terrific husband and such wonderful friends as all of you. I look forward to sharing more laughs and good times with all of you in the future!

LOVE, Diane

P.S. Many of you are the key contact person in the many groups that I enjoy being a member of... I never realized what a social butterfly I was until I had to compose this email! Please pass this message on to anyone else in the group I may have missed as I've had a lot on my mind and if I forgot anyone - it is unintentional.

CHAPTER 30

A few words from my Spouse

My wife is a very special person who has somehow managed to turn adversity into a positive in her very challenging life. It is amazing how she is able to get through the very tough times while having a positive attitude about life and the simple things that we should always cherish. Despite waging a very difficult war with cancer she is able to start the day with a smile on her face and an attitude that makes everyone around her feel that life is good.

Diane and I have always been somewhat counterparts to each other. She always looks at what can go right and I am always there to say what could possibly go wrong. I worry about things and she is always there to say everything will be fine. Her attitude meets each new day with the challenge of "what can I do now that is interesting and will stimulate my mind?"

As I write this, we are waiting to hear from the doctor about whether or not a mass that was discovered in a pelvic ultrasound is a new cancer that she will have to fight once again. Not once have I heard her complain or act like this is the end of the world. Instead, she is out starting her day playing tennis, participating in other social activities and making our home a wonderful, positive place to be in. If it was me, I would probably crawl into a hole and hide. This is not my wife. She doesn't give it any thought. She has the type of personality that loves storms.

I think that no matter what obstacles she faces that it would be done with enthusiasm and optimism. There is an inner strength in her soul that is impossible to break down. No fight that she isn't willing to take on. I even have a confidence that if I was to leave this lovely earth that she would continue to forge ahead with great gusto.

My own feeling is that this type of person is a rarity and that is why I think so many people have encouraged her to write about her life and where she gets her inner strength.

The lessons of life are many and I hope that what Diane has set as an example can inspire others to better deal with the many battles that confront them during this life on earth.

Sweetheart, you are the sunshine of my life.

CHAPTER 31

Marijuana

It wasn't until I had cancer that I ever tried marijuana. Marijuana had been available to me when I was growing up but I refused to try it for all the good reasons that we know. Such as:

1) Marijuana is illegal
2) Marijuana is considered a gate way drug leading to more addictive drugs
3) Marijuana is expensive
4) Marijuana contains a mind altering drug (THC) that may affect your ability to drive or make decisions

Point made, enough said about reasons not to enjoy marijuana. Once it became known that I had breast cancer, someone (a friend who will remain anonymous) offered me some marijuana. I gave it some serious consideration, and at first refused to try marijuana. This friend thought it might help me with nausea and appetite loss from the chemo treatments. To be honest I never experienced nausea, just a metallic taste in my mouth. As for my appetite, I'm afraid I fell into the trap of over eating as though every meal was going to be my last. But I had heard rumors about marijuana creating a sense of peace, stimulating your appetite, being a sleep aid and that it would help to spice up your sex life. I know these qualities sound too good to be true.

Well, after a lifetime of avoiding all drug use, I tried marijuana and here's what I experienced. It was fun! I felt happy and uplifted, yes – high is a good description of the state of mind marijuana put me in. I experienced a feeling of relaxation and an increased sex drive. My husband found it increased his libido too! When I smoked marijuana it turned out to be a blast; I certainly had the shits and giggles. I don't like inhaling smoke; it hurts my lungs and makes me cough. So when I was offered a marijuana edible in the form of a cookie, I tried it and found it preferable to smoking.

Our national government continues to treat marijuana as an illegal drug though more and more states are allowing medicinal marijuana prescriptions and recently the state of Colorado made the recreational use of marijuana, legal. I realize there are a lot of issues that have to be worked out regarding the control of a legal and/or illegal drug such as marijuana. People who have been fined or incarcerated for possession of marijuana have issues that will have to be addressed by our government. But I think there is hope that marijuana and the THC element that makes a person feel 'better' will become an acceptable part of cancer and other diseases prescribed treatment plan.

Here are my thoughts, newbie that I am, on the use of marijuana:

I prefer Edibles over Smoking marijuana.

Marijuana helps in dealing with cancer and/or other serious health conditions.

My suggestion is that unless you really need it, save the enjoyment of marijuana for special occasions. Don't overdo marijuana – moderation is the key in maintaining a low tolerance.

The time has come for people and our government to reconsider their stance and change the laws regarding marijuana use. To date no one has yet overdosed and died from marijuana use whereas many have died from alcohol abuse – a legal substance whose taxes go to support the operation of our state and federal government. When you compare the guidelines and laws for the use of alcohol and the taxes imposed on alcoholic spirits to the potential income from the marijuana industry it seems like a no-brainer that the time for legalizing and thereby taxing marijuana has come.

Who knew that having cancer and all the stress associated with it would lead me to try to relax, experience marijuana and enjoy unexpected pleasure? Again the comparison I have been making in this book about how experiencing sour helps you to recognize and appreciate the sweet in life comes to mind. I highly endorse utilizing the benefits of marijuana in coping with cancer or any other life threatening disease.

CHAPTER 32

Summary: Appreciate the 'Good Things in Life'

Top 10 ideas to reflect on every day in order to overcome adversity and to get you through this difficult time

1) Interact with nature.
2) Become more active, get outside and exercise - jog, play tennis, swim etc.
3) Tell your favorite person that you love them or how much you care about them, now!
4) Watch or read something that makes you laugh. Laughter is the best medicine.

5) Call a relative - mother, father, and child.... reach out!
6) Go for a walk with friends. Many problems are solved while walking, talking etc.
7) Break out a sketch pad or camera and draw, paint, sculpt – be creative!
8) Step outside, close your eyes, smell flowers, feel a breeze, sunshine, smile and give thanks!
9) Indulge in your favorite vice and have great sex!
10) Write your memoir, count your blessings and be grateful for the time you've had on Earth.

Acknowledgements

I would like to recognize and thank all the medical staff and doctors of the Florida Hospital system who helped me with my various surgeries ranging from lumpectomy, chemotherapy, radiation, monitoring my mammograms, double mastectomy, genetic counseling and testing, breast reconstruction, complete hysterectomy and plastic surgery.

Thank you!

John T. Nonweiler, M.D.
Alan Keller, M.D. F.A.C.S.
Lee Zehngebot, M.D.
Michael Sombeck, M.D.
Nafiza Tejpar, M.D. F.A.C.S.
Giselle B. Ghurani, M.D., FACOG
Nefertari Donerson, MS
Aileen Caceras, M.D. MPH, FACOG

Kendall K. Peters, M.D.
Olga Ivanov, M.D., F.A.C.S.
Jennie Yoon, M.D.
Tara Udelson PA
Amber Bruens PA

Cynthia Buffington, PhD – my former roommate and fellow walker on the road to wellness

Joanne Wilmot – who shares her friendship and life wisdom with me

Libby Bumpus – being one of your 'bestest' friends is an honor

Pam Smith – my tolerant bridge partner and fellow breast cancer survivor

KT Budde-Jones – fellow triple negative buddy and breast cancer researcher without compare

Lynn Bottger – USTA Tennis Pro who taught me to play good doubles tennis and encouraged me to write this book

Kim Kirschner – your knowledge on making healthy choices is amazing. Thank you for setting a good example and showing the way to a healthier lifestyle

Joanne Lyman – thanks for all the encouragement and help

Valerie Crabtree – we have fought many battles together

Tuesday Morning Walkers – You helped us get through the worst of times – a friend in need … are friends indeed!

In addition, I would like to thank many friends and family members too numerous to mention individually – you know who you are! You never asked for thanks, just how you could help me. I am sincerely grateful for the good advice, hugs, and walks around the pond and on the beach. Your smiles of encouragement, good karma and great camaraderie are appreciated more than I can describe.

I would like to thank my sons Robert, Nicholas and Jack, their significant others Courtney and Cassie and especially my husband Chris – you have been pillars of support to me in my hours of need! I love you all so much… you give me reason and determination to live!

The End

About the Author

Diane Finney is an award winning writer whose short stories have been published in *Not Everyone's Cup of Tea: An Interesting and Entertaining History of Malice Domestic's First 25*

years. Diane has served as President of the Garden Club of Celebration and for many years has written articles for the local newspaper. Diane graduated from the University of Minnesota with a BA degree in Anthropology. She's valued every work experience ranging from being a library page, Coordinator of Volunteers at the U of MN Landscape Arboretum, travel reservationist, Realtor and serving as an Osceola County Planning Commissioner.

Diane has been a member of the National League of American Pen Women, the Cape Cod Writer's Center, Sisters in Crime, Romance Writers of America, Mystery Writers of America and The Loft. She's attended many writing conferences including Malice Domestic, Left Coast Crime, RWA, SleuthFest and Bouchercon. When she's not writing, Diane enjoys photography and creating botanical art. She sincerely hopes this book will be helpful to people dealing with cancer – Diane's only just begun working on her Bucket List and she looks forward to accomplishing those goals!

About the Publisher
MacGuffin Press

MacGuffin Press was created in 2014 by Diane Finney. The name MacGuffin was chosen for the Press because the MacGuffin is a plot device described and used by Alfred Hitchcock - to motivate the characters and advance the story. The MacGuffin is known to be the "object of great desire" such as the statue of the bird in the Maltese Falcon or the papers of transport in Casablanca.

www.ingramcontent.com/pod-product-compliance
Lightning Source LLC
Chambersburg PA
CBHW071507040426
42444CB00008B/1530